Mom's MAGNAVOX

A story about
family, growing up
and, of course...
The Pittsburgh Pirates

Ben DiCola

Mom's Magnavox by Ben DiCola

Copyright ©2023 by Ben DiCola

ISBN: 9798376853313
Printed in the United States of America

Published in the United States of America

Cover by Ryan Humbert
Project Management by Inkling Creative Strategies

> To John:
> Thanks so much! Beat 'em Bucs!
> Ben.

For Mom and Dad

Table of Contents

Mom's Magnavox 1
Mazeroski's Home Run Still Unites a Region 9
The Brotherhood of Baseball 14
Italian Saturdays 21
The Man Cave 27
Rain, Rain, Go Away 31
Misfit in the Ranks 36
Baseball Cards Forever 42
Men in Black 48
A Baseball Lesson in Civil Rights 53
A Whole New Meaning to Opening Day 59
Opening Day Heartbreak .64
Baseball and Race Relations 71
Lost Ticket 76
Practically at Forbes 89
Hot August Night 96
Bradenton-Sarasota Calling! 101
Rennie Stennett 107
The Phone Call 110
The Coronavirus Curveball 118
Take Me Out to the Ballgame . . . Someday! 122
Tomorrow Isn't Promised 127
What? No Baseball? 133
A Kid at Sixty-Five 138
Baseball, Marriage, and Family 143
Thanks, Dad! 147
This Old House 151
Acknowledgments 157
About the Author 159

Author's Note

The following essays were originally composed between 2015 and 2022 as part of my blog, *Pittsburgh Pirates Memories*. While some essays remain as relevant as they were when I first wrote them, others capture particular moments in time and thus include information that is now outdated. Baseball has returned from its hiatus of the COVID-19 pandemic, the lockout of 2022 has been resolved, and, for better or worse, the Cleveland Indians are now the Guardians.

In addition, some of the Pirates and baseball luminaries mentioned in this book have since passed on.

It is my hope that these essays illustrate not simply an era in baseball history that meant so much to me growing up, but also how the game and the events surrounding it continue to evolve in the present.

—Ben DiCola

Mom's Magnavox

Mom at Christmas in 1962.

Mom's Magnavox

One thing that made baseball so great in decades gone by was listening to the game on the radio. The radio and baseball were perfect marriage partners. There was Jack Buck on KMOX St. Louis, Ernie Harwell on WJR in Detroit, and Harry Kalas on KYW in Philadelphia. Jimmy Dudley was the Voice of the Cleveland Indians for two decades, and Dodger Stadium will always resonate with the voice of Vin Scully.

Scully was inexorably linked with Dodgers' baseball for sixty-seven seasons in Brooklyn and Los Angeles. Nearly every fan brought his scorecard and a portable radio to Chavez Ravine just to hear Scully's unique and unparalleled analysis of how the simplest pop fly to right center field met a leathered mitt just before sundown. Even the commercials were memorable. "Kahn's: it's the wiener the world awaited!"

My favorite baseball announcer was Bob Prince on KDKA in Pittsburgh doing the Pirates' broadcasts. Prince would announce a close play at first base as "Bang-bang" or as "Close as fuzz on a tick's ear," or "He was out by a gnat's eyelash." A big, strong Pirates slugger like Bob Robertson "could hit a ball out of any park, including Yellowstone!" If he were an overpowering pitcher, Prince would say, "This guy can throw a strawberry through a locomotive!"

Lanny Frattare replaced Prince as "Voice of the Pirates" in 1976. I used to enjoy his commentary and wit as well. "Go Ball, Get Outta Here!" was Lanny's classic radio call of a Pirates' home run. He also educated us that contrary to popular belief, just because a player made a great play in the field to end one inning didn't mean he always came to bat to lead off the next.

Lanny also entertained us with his "All Presidential Team" during rain delays. He had

Whitey Ford on the mound and Gary Carter catching behind the plate. Lou Clinton was one of the outfielders, and there was sure to be a Washington and Jefferson in the lineup. Above all else, his shortstop was always John Kennedy of the old Washington Senators. JFK was Lanny's favorite president.

On September 16, 1975, I was listening to the Pirates on my mother's Magnavox radio when Pirates' second baseman Rennie Stennett went seven for seven, slapping and spraying seven base hits into the blades of grass at Chicago's Wrigley Field on a crisp autumn day on the city's North Side. Pittsburgh went on to a 22–0 shellacking of the Cubs.

I knew I was listening to history that day. There was no ESPN, no Baseball Tonight highlights. There were no Facebook or Twitter accounts lighting up. No hand-held updates on Android phones. Ah, but there was baseball on the radio. That you could count on.

Radios in our house held special significance. Each person in the family had their very own. Mine was encased in brown leather, featured AM and FM bands, and had a silver antenna, which I needed to extend at night to bring in Pirates' games on KDKA from the

Mom's Magnavox

west coast. Sometimes I went to bed, but somehow "forgot" to tell my parents that I was lying there with earplugs in my ears, listening to the Pirates play the Dodgers with the first pitch delivered at 11:05 p.m. Eastern time. Yes, there was school the next day.

I loved my radio, but it lacked the power output of my Mom's Magnavox. Trouble was, the Magnavox was the family radio. Mom listened to it and kept it tuned to local stations for news and weather reports. It was not purchased to listen to baseball games, and I knew better than to just turn it on to listen to a pre-game warm-up show. I knew to ask first, and if I asked politely, Mom would usually allow me to dial in 1020-AM, KDKA.

That's what I remember most: asking permission to listen to a ballgame on the family radio.

I recall one night when the Pirates played the San Francisco Giants at Candlestick Park. The Pirates were staging a rally with the bases loaded, and future Hall of Fame slugger Willie Stargell was striding toward home plate. I was in the kitchen listening on Mom's Magnavox. The signal was strong and clear. I'd miss this uprising if I were listening to the game on my smaller radio.

In an adjacent room we called the pantry, Mom was busy sewing. She had been an accomplished seamstress for years, mending many garments for friends, altar linens, and even vestments for priests who were friends of the family. Mom would often start up her Singer sewing machine late at night when everyone else had gone to bed. It was her relaxation time with the daily house cleaning and cooking chores behind her.

I seriously doubt she knew the Pirates were playing on the west coast. But I knew, of course, and that meant only me and Mom were still awake when everyone else had now retired for the evening.

When the count was full on Stargell at three balls and two strikes, then came the pause. Everything fell silent at the belt before the San Francisco pitcher would deliver the payoff pitch.

As Prince's inflection rose in anticipation of the pitch, Mom called out to me from the pantry room. "Are they at an important part of the game?" she asked.

"Well, sort of," I said sheepishly, feeling guilty because a 3–2 bases-loaded fastball was about to be thrown at the exact same time my Mom was finishing a hem in a skirt. You see, if my Mom were to run the sewing machine while the game's turning point was about to unfold, it would cause severe static on the Magnavox. I would miss what was about to happen. But just like the Giants' pitcher, Mom paused, too.

"Stargell swings and rips a ball down the right field line . . . this is going to score a pair of runs!" announced Prince in his gravelly tone of voice. The Pirates had taken the lead on Stargell's RBI double. After the Giants manager came to take his pitcher out of the game, Mom started up the Singer, and static erupted on the Magnavox. At least it was after the turning point in the game.

Certainly, my Mom did far more important things for me than pausing on her sewing machine one summer night so I could hear the climatic hit in a baseball game. But often, the most significant memories of someone you dearly loved are from the simplest moments. One pitch, one inning, one game.

I don't remember the score of that game. I think the Pirates won, but the game itself holds no importance today like it did the night my Mom stopped sewing so I could hear what happened.

Baseball on the radio really does conjure up classic memories . . . even ones that were never broadcast, or that you ever could have imagined.

Mazeroski's Home Run Still Unites a Region

Some things get better with time. Wine is the first that comes to mind, but in Pittsburgh each October, there's another vintage that continues to grow in legend. Every October 13, a small crowd (sometimes a big one) gathers in the city's Oakland neighborhood to commemorate the most extraordinary moment in Pittsburgh's sports history.

That was the day Bill Mazeroski, a young Pirates second baseman, clobbered a leadoff home run in the bottom of the ninth inning in the seventh game of the 1960 World Series at Forbes Field to defeat the heavily favored

New York Yankees 10–9. Many baseball historians insist it remains the greatest World Series game ever played.

When the informal yet nostalgic crowd convenes each year, they listen to the entire play-by-play broadcast of that game. They can thank two people for being able to relive the Pirates' stunning victory that autumn afternoon at precisely 3:36 p.m. Eastern time: Saul Finkelstein and Herb Soltman.

Finklestein, a Pittsburgh native, discovered the audio broadcast of Game Seven in the basement of the late Bing Crosby's home. Crosby had held ownership in the Pirates franchise at the time of the 1960 World Series. Forbes Field is long gone, but the entire outfield wall, including the spot where Mazeroski's home run cleared in left field, remains intact. The flag pole, which in those days sat in deep centerfield, has also been preserved. Centerfield at Forbes was 457 feet deep, and not many baseballs were going to travel frequent flyer miles.

Finklestein would sit under the flag pole and listen to a cassette recording of the 1960 classic every year. Eventually, local author Jim O'Brien realized what he was doing. "O'Brien spread the word to the local press that he was sitting there listening to this game every year," recalled Soltman, age eighty-one, who was twenty-five when he attended Game Seven in 1960. "We started getting people to come out about 1992 to listen to the entire game again."

Soltman, who chairs a promotional group called the "Game Seven Gang," added, "We average about two hundred people a year. But in 2010 [the fiftieth anniversary of the Pirates' historic victory], we drew about sixteen hundred people."

Fans gather in a park-like setting across the street from a University of Pittsburgh campus building each October 13. Hot dogs and crackerjacks are sold—though not at 1960 prices—and patrons bring lawn chairs to relive the call made by the late Chuck Thompson on the radio. The university took over the property after the ballpark was razed in 1972.

"I sat about ten rows up behind the Pirates' dugout on the first base side," Soltman said. "I paid $7.70 for a box seat." The attendance at Forbes Field that day was 36,683, although thousands more now claim they were present when Maz's blast sailed over the brick wall into the city's Schenley Park area.

The Yankees beat the Pirates in every other conceivable way except in what mattered most—winning Game Seven. New York, with its famed lineup featuring Mickey Mantle, Roger Maris, and Yogi Berra outscored Pittsburgh, 55–27 in the series. The Bronx Bombers also hit .338 as a team to the Pirates' .256, outhit them 91–60, and posted a lower-earned run average (3.54 to Pittsburgh's 7.11). In addition, the Yankees had the Series' Most Valuable Player in second baseman Bobby Richardson.

Soltman welcomes the crowd each year and addresses them from a podium. The national anthem and the seventh-inning stretch rendition of "Take Me Out to the Ballgame" are still observed by those in attendance. The podium where Soltman stands is draped with bunting from the 1960 classic. "William Tingler gave me the bunting from the game that day," Soltman added.

While Forbes Field, along with many players and the managers of the 1960 World Series (Pittsburgh's Danny Murtaugh and New York's Casey Stengel) are no longer with us, Game Seven will live on for years to come.

The remaining section of Forbes Field's left to left-center wall where fans gather to relive Game 7 of the 1960 World Series.

The Brotherhood of Baseball

Trust is the most elusive virtue of all. We trust the life partners we choose at the altar of matrimony, yet the divorce rate in America is well over fifty percent. We trust our siblings, priests, ministers, and even Uber drivers and pizza delivery boys. But all too often, they also have betrayed our trust.

So, who can we place our trust in? Would you believe a baseball fan? While you chuckle and scoff at this notion, allow me to provide you with some real-life, first-hand examples.

On my most recent trip to Bradenton, Florida, which the Pittsburgh Pirates have called their spring training home since 1969, I was dining at The Beach House on Bradenton Beach when two Pittsburgh Pirates fans walked in, easily identifiable by their black and white caps and shirts. The Pirates had played the Twins that day at LECOM Park. I knew the game had been played but didn't know the outcome, as my phone had run out of minutes. Assuming these fans had attended the game, I approached their table to find out the final score.

"The Pirates won, 1–0," one of them said.

I immediately asked, "Who pitched?"

If you are not a baseball fan yet are reading this book intently, you need to realize that this is a most critical question. If the final score had been 6–2 or 8–3, then there would be no need to ask who pitched. But if the final tally is 1–0, that margin is paper-thin, and the man who pitched takes center stage in terms of the game's importance. After all, he held the opponent scoreless.

"Chase De Jong," the other man noted. In the end, De Jong didn't make the club coming out of spring training. (Considering the fate of the team's pitching staff, perhaps he should have!) Nonetheless, a five-minute conversation between myself and the two fans ensued, even though I had never seen them before, and they certainly did not know me. It's quite possible that I would have nothing in common with either man, other than that we root for the same baseball team.

Let's dissect this further, shall we? Would you strike up a conversation with a total stranger because you both drive a pickup? Or an Equinox? Well, yes, you could. But it's far less likely, especially if you don't know the person at all. Would you go out of your way to talk to the person ahead of you in the grocery store checkout line simply because they bought the same brand of orange juice or coffee that you purchased? Again, yes, you could. But the other person would likely wonder why you are even asking. So what? Where does the conversation go after you've established that each of you prefers Maxwell House coffee in cans?

Yet, this exchange on Bradenton Beach with the Gulf of Mexico serving as a heavenly visual backdrop continued. Not only did we discuss De Jong's performance that day, but we also evaluated the Pirates' starting rotation overall, pitchers the team used to have that were now pitching elsewhere, the team's record in spring training, who was currently injured and couldn't play, and when the first game of the season was scheduled.

These questions and subsequent answers were expected. Nobody was taken aback by it. It was as though the three of us were all in the same high school graduating class. We were not, of course, as I could readily surmise by looking at the two men that each was at least twenty years younger than I am. Maybe this is the "male bonding" concept we often hear about, but it's clear that because of baseball, and only because of it, the three of us could engage in this non-planned, unrehearsed discourse.

To further illustrate the bond of baseball brotherhood, consider this transaction between myself and Shane Vecchio, a fellow Pirates fan and a Pittsburgh resident. The power of social media allowed the doors of friendship to swing wide open between us. I didn't know Shane from Moses or Joshua, but through the convenience of the internet and the commonality of being Pirates fans who met on a team Facebook page, we became friends.

It was my good fortune that Shane happened to have a rare 1960 Pirates World Series program from when Pittsburgh upset the heavily favored New York Yankees that fall. He posted it online and was willing to accept a sale to the first responder—who turned out to be me. I asked Shane how much he wanted for the storied program that went for fifty cents over six decades ago. His asking price was one hundred and twenty-five dollars. He told me it remained in good condition.

Now, here is where the formidable bond of trust comes in. It became clear that Shane had to trust a person like me, whom he had never seen or met, to mail him a check for one hundred and twenty-five dollars. I, too, had to trust someone I had never met—a person I only knew through a computer screen—to send me what he claimed was a 1960 Pirates World Series program that he further confirmed was in "good condition." We exchanged a few messages centered on this point, but we both knew the other would come through with his end of the bargain.

How did we know that?

We knew because baseball fans have an unshakable foundation, a firm resolve that comes from the lifelong loyalty of following a sports team, good or bad, successful or not. Would I trust anyone else with a transaction online? No, because the brotherhood of man wouldn't be attached to it. Outside of the unity among baseball fans, that bond of trust doesn't exist.

The 1960 World Series program was indeed in very good condition, and Shane Vecchio did indeed receive his one hundred and twenty-five dollars from me. What he did with it is his business. I know what I did with the program. It rests comfortably on the first shelf of my Pirates baseball shrine in my sports den. The ads in the program are as startling as the content. One message advertises Schick razor blades. Another promotes Philco radios—"now available in stereo."

There are highlights of the Pirates' 1960 season, a picture of Dodgers pitcher Don Drysdale lunging to tag Pirates shortstop Dick Groat, and a full history of the World Series players' shares in previous years. I didn't know which was more shocking to the eye—the fact that the year before, in 1959, the individual players' winning share on the Los Angeles Dodgers was $11,231.18, or that there was a full-page congratulatory ad honoring the 1960 Pirates from the Republican presidential ticket that year, Richard Nixon and Henry Cabot Lodge.

All I know for sure is that trust can still thrive between people. Being a baseball fan may not be the only way to achieve it, but without question, it's an excellent start.

The original 1960 World Series souvenir program I purchased from Shane Vecchio, courtesy of the Brotherhood of Baseball! (Photo by Charlie Edmisten)

Italian Saturdays

Growing up, Saturday was by far the best day of the week. No school, and in the summertime, barbecue picnics, sleeping in until eleven o'clock, and baseball on television. Even when there was work to be done, Saturday was still a day to behold.

However, my mom hated Saturdays, unlike my dad, who loved them. With Dad, work always had a reward attached to the end of it. The distribution of labor went like this: Dad would trim the hedges that separated our property line from the neighbor's while I mowed the yard. Because mowing was a full-morning chore, my taking on this job gave him time to finish the hedges and attend to other yard work, which he would not have been able to do had he devoted all his time to the task.

When the chores were completed, it was lunchtime. Looking back now, I think he planned it that way. I guess he figured if we started in the yard around ten o'clock or ten-thirty, we'd be hungry by the time we finished. Boy, was he right!

So in we came from outside, and by now, it was one or one-thirty, and Mom was livid. "I hate Saturdays," she used to say. You have to understand that Italian women of her generation held the kitchen as their private domain. This was her turf, and on Saturdays, we were completely invading her world. What was she to do once Dad brought out the skillets to fry up sausage and peppers? As for me, I would clean up and tune into the NBC pre-game show, as Baseball's Game of the Week was about to come on: the Pirates vs. the Giants from Forbes Field.

As I watched the preshow and prepared my scorecard, my nostrils inhaled heaven. The scent of sausage and peppers wafting from the kitchen one room over into the living room where I was sitting was intoxicating. We didn't have a smoke alarm in the 1960s, but the smoke rising to the ceiling would have set off alarms for three city blocks had we owned one. At the sight of the smoke, Mom, in a classic Italian woman gesture, raised her arms and said, "Oooh, My God!" She didn't relish the idea of having her drapes and linens in adjacent rooms smelling of thick smoke from a sausage and pepper skillet.

Then I began to consider the unthinkable . . . could my dad be as good a cook as my mom? How many kids could say that? I could because, with no disrespect to my mom, my dad could have been a chef. I mean, the man could cook! I remember sausage and pepper sandwiches and baseball on Saturdays like it was yesterday.

Often, Mom packed me school lunches (Dad did not) that included two thick-crusted slices of Italian bread around sausage, peppers, and eggplant. I was in the third grade, and no kid at school ate sandwiches like that at lunchtime. Nobody! They'd get the standard slice of bologna and cheese with a dab of mustard. The bread was evenly sliced and cornered. It could easily fit into a sandwich container.

Mine? Forget it! I'd take one bite into it, and sausage and one green pepper would squirt out the side while my molars desperately tried to tear the thick-crusted Italian bread. The bread was fresh, but it was as thick as shoe leather. The other kids would laugh. "Ben, are you having dinner or what? Do you need a knife?"

At the time, I thought everyone ate this way. If I had these kinds of sandwiches, they did too, right? Uh, not quite! But we always think our way of doing things is the standard way, don't we? We are the norm, and everyone else is out of step.

As the years have passed, I find it amusing that nearly everyone falls into the following categories when it comes to Italian heritage or tradition. One, you wish you were Italian. Two, you know someone who is. And three, you start gesturing and eating like one.

People have always asked me for Italian recipes. This is particularly hilarious to Italians because we don't have recipes. I never even saw my grandmother refer to an index card on how to prepare a dish. It's all in your head and your hands. My mom made pasta

Fagioli long before it became a popular dish at places like Carrabba's. She used to tell us it was a peasant's dinner. The workers in the fields in Italy ate it because it was relatively inexpensive to prepare. Today, it is considered a luxury item on American menus.

You think Dad followed a recipe for those sausage and pepper lunches he made for the two of us on Saturdays? No way. He already knew what he was doing before he pulled out the skillet. My mom didn't like surrendering her turf, but he certainly was good at it. Dad took over the kitchen on Sundays, too, when he made another Italian classic: spaghetti and meatballs, along with sausage, chicken, and sometimes hock or spare ribs that he'd use in the sauce. My Lord was that good!

Funny thing is, my mom could make it equally as well, as she did on Thursdays. We always had sauce and some form of a macaroni product on Thursdays and Sundays. It was as perennial as church on Sundays or flowers in the spring.

But Saturdays belonged to me and my dad. We took over the yard, and we took over the kitchen. I learned to cook from both my parents, and it is one of the greatest gifts they passed along to me. As a matter of fact, I think I'll go home right now and start up some sausage with green and red peppers. Oh yes, I can make it too. But it's not quite the same, is it? You see, we are only children once, and besides, today we have a smoke alarm.

Dad was excellent on the stove or on the grill.

The Man Cave

A while back, I moved into a new two-bedroom apartment. With that comes my obligatory sports room that displays hundreds of sports artifacts, photographs, articles, books, and assorted memorabilia. For some reason, men need this. It is commonly called a "Man Cave."

Ever notice that you never hear about a "Woman Cave?" Why is that? Couldn't they also have a sports room with shelves containing historical sports memories? Of course. Or, depending on the woman, she could have a room devoted to Maybelline products, two hundred pairs of heels, the history of Barbie and Ken, or what to wear on your wedding day.

Maybe some women do have these things. I don't know. I live alone, so I'm the wrong person to ask. But even if they do, nobody refers to such a room as a Woman Cave. Maybe men need a space such as this because they need to escape. They have a stronger, inherent need to recapture their youth. I mean, why else would I have a picture of Pittsburgh Pirates manager Danny Murtaugh pinching the cheek of Bill Mazeroski after Mazeroski hit his historic home run in Game Seven of the 1960 World Series, giving the Pirates a victory over the fabled New York Yankees? And why would I have an old Wheaties box with Roberto Clemente's picture on the front of it? And does any woman pay one hundred and twenty-five dollars for a 1960 World Series program to put in her cave that was sold for fifty cents at Forbes Field?

It's possible, I guess, but I seriously doubt it. Men and women have always been different creatures, and nothing accentuates this more than a man having a 1960 World Series program that contains ads for cigarettes and a woman owning a collection of

Maybelline eyeliner.

Seriously though, I'm proud of my man cave. There are a ton of memories in there, and to the right person, I could probably charge an admission price. As James Earl Jones once said so eloquently, "It represents all that is good and can be again."

I also have a banner listing all the Pirates' World Series championships: 1909, 1925, 1960, 1971, and 1979. As the years pass, of course, fewer and fewer people can relate to these memories because they simply were not yet born. I sure am glad I was around to see it. Okay, maybe not 1909 or 1925, but I recall the other years. There is also a plaque in the man cave noting the first-ever World Series played on October 1, 1903, between the Pirates and the Boston Red Sox. (No, I wasn't around to witness that either.)

The most important aspect of having a man cave, though, is to announce to others who you are, what you remember, and what you cherish. Even though my memories may not be yours, that doesn't mean I can't bring you through my door and share them with you. Perhaps it will help inspire you to collect and someday display all that you cherish, all that you hold dear, and all that you remember from your childhood and adolescence.

What is most important of all to remember is this: You didn't grow old because you stopped being a kid. You stopped being a kid, and you grew old.

My shrine at home dedicated to the Pittsburgh Pirates.

Rain, Rain, Go Away

On my most recent trip to Pittsburgh, I combined two visits that normally would not go together. First, I went to the Roberto Clemente baseball museum, a must-see for any baseball follower. After that, I stopped off to see my cousin Mary Lou and her husband, Dan, in nearby Greensburg, Pennsylvania, about an hour east of Pittsburgh. Mary Lou and Dan watch baseball the way most guys watch commercials for hairspray.

The Clemente Museum is a fitting tribute to the man who elegantly played right field for the Pittsburgh Pirates for eighteen seasons and tragically lost his life in a plane crash off the coast of Puerto Rico while aiding earthquake victims in Nicaragua on December 31, 1972. The Clemente story and legacy honoring the first Latin American baseball player elected to baseball's Hall of Fame has been well-documented and chronicled.

On the other hand, there was Mary Lou and Dan's reaction to my telling them about the Clemente story, the museum itself, and baseball in general. Ever notice what an interesting reaction you get inside when you're discussing something with others that you know they know little or nothing about? Admit it. It makes you feel pretty good, right? Even if they know more than you about the stock market, global warming, or the next general election, you know more than them about baseball! See? Everything evens out.

This also happened to be my birthday weekend, so a trip to the museum to see the collection and memories of my favorite professional athlete of all time and a chance to spend some quality time with my cousin tempered my enthusiasm over turning sixty-five, even though I'm told I don't look a day over fifty-three. Sounds good to me!

Mary Lou and Dan insisted on taking

me to dinner. The hometown Pirates game that day against the Milwaukee Brewers had been delayed by rain, so even though the big screens had the Pirates telecast on, there was no game to see. This, however, ended up being a good thing because the dinner conversation did not center on whether the Pirates could catch the first-place Cubs in the National League Central pennant race. Remember, these guys are not baseball fans. Instead, they talked to me about much less important topics, such as my general health, how my sisters were doing, whether I had found a Medicare supplement yet, and yes, maybe even global warming.

At least I could listen and respond to them accordingly. Had the game not been delayed and action on the field was taking place, I'd have been peering around their shoulders, straining to see if a line drive off Starling Marte's bat would fall in for a two-run single. Had the game been underway, I'd have been forced to nod as if I were listening to them and acting as though I were engaged in the discussion. But without the game going on, they now had my undivided attention.

It makes you feel so much more adult-like, doesn't it? By not watching a silly game that no one will remember next season, or even next week, I could now fully concentrate on whether to select a Medicare supplement that includes coverage for my prescription drugs and how long I should put off taking social security.

I felt like a grown-up. Oh my God . . . *I felt sixty-five.*

But in the end, I was ready for them to take off that tarp. Start the game. You're going to tell me the anticipation of whether a batted ball will lead to two runs isn't important in life?

People who aren't baseball fans are some of my best friends. It is not life or death. The winning team will not pay your mortgage. They won't select a Medicare plan for you, and they won't solve global warming. I fully understand Mary Lou, Dan, and the thousands of others who do not keep up with baseball. They are undoubtedly better at adulthood than I'll ever be. They have made important decisions I might not ever face. But baseball is one thing I have that many others don't have and will never understand . . . even when the weather stops the game.

I'm sixty-five years old, but so what? Rain, rain, go away. I want to feel like a kid again!

My cousin Mary Lou Andrews (second from left), her husband Dan (center), friends, and me (far right) enjoying lunch at Primanti Brothers in Pittsburgh.

Misfit in the Ranks

So, here I am: a guest in someone else's house. A visitor. Depending on where I'm sitting, I'm someone who doesn't belong. This is how it is when you're a Pittsburgh Pirates fan sitting in the home of the Cleveland Indians. A sea of red and blue drowns out my black and gold attire. No, I'm not the only one, as there are other Pirates fans scattered throughout Progressive Field near Lake Erie. But it looks like I'm the only one in my row cheering for the visiting team.

It looks that way because it is that way.

It's a strange and unwelcome feeling. Think about it. Unless you lose, you stand out like a sore thumb. Like a Republican at a

Democratic convention. Or my personal favorite—like a French whore in church on Sunday.

Well, you get the point. I'm outnumbered in this environment. I suppose it is rude when you think about it. I'm clapping and cheering while the rest of my row, along with the other seventy percent of those in attendance, are stone silent when the Pirates behind Starling Marte, Josh Bell, and Gregory Polanco all clobber home runs during a 9–4 victory over the home team, the beloved Indians. I am taking joy and pleasure in the fact that the Bucs (a nickname for the Pirates) are getting all the spoils, even though it is taking place at someone else's residence.

Imagine this in any other area of life. Imagine going into your next-door neighbor's house, eating their English muffins, brewing and drinking their coffee, maybe making a ham and cheese sandwich for lunch, then sitting back and enjoying it all on their sofa. All this while the host welcomes you through the front door and watches you enjoy yourself while they sit and suffer and get nothing.

This happens a lot in baseball. The home team certainly does not always win. They do not always get the English muffins. But this is permitted in baseball. Not only are you allowed to be a rude guest in someone else's house, but you are expected to show up and be rude in someone else's house. After all, do you think they won't want to be rude to you the next time you host them? Stop by and eat your English muffins and make themselves a ham and cheese sandwich at your expense while you watch helplessly? If you don't think so, you're naive.

What made this night even more troubling for me was that I rode up with three other people, all of whom were rooting for the Indians and none of whom were wearing any semblance of black and gold attire.

Oh, the perils of interleague play in Major League Baseball! There is a groundswell of folks who want interleague play abolished from the baseball scene—no more English muffins for you. I can appreciate that, as I am now being insulted, verbally attacked, and booed traveling south on Interstate 77 on the drive home. These three felt robbed. One was my sister, who hadn't seen her Indians play in two years because she was recovering from brain surgery. Now I really felt like a jerk!

Let's face it. The Indians have a better

team than the Pirates right now. I'm sure I'd think I'd beat a team in my home park in a year when my team will play October baseball and the losing team will be home watching from their recliners. (Maybe even munching on English muffins, who knows?)

And now, when I can finally see a ballgame, when I have finally regained my strength and stamina, when I can finally walk the concourse and reach my seat, I must witness the much-hated Pittsburgh Pirates hit three home runs and win 9–4? Something is wrong with this picture. I waited two years to see *that*?

I'm sure that's what she must have been thinking. I know that's how I'd think.

But as Tom Hanks told us in the film *A League of Their Own*, there's no crying in baseball. I'm told it's all cyclical. When I'm watching the Indians play in October, I'll be the one crying because the Pirates won't be playing. My family and friends often remind me that the Indians haven't won a World Series since 1948. Well, I can say the Pirates haven't won a World Series since 1979. But you see, no one cares because there's no crying in baseball.

So, when you have the chance to grab the English muffins and ham and cheese sandwiches as a guest in someone else's house, do it while you can. After all, sometimes you get the bear. But sometimes, the bear will also get you. You can count on that!

Pitching to my sister Chris on our driveway sometime in the early 1960s.

Baseball Cards Forever

One night, I was looking through my collection of 2,500 baseball cards dating back to the mid-1950s. I came across a 1966 Topps card of Phillies pitcher Jim Bunning. I remember always liking the pose Bunning took in his '66 photo, following through with his right-handed delivery. I recalled that Bunning pitched a perfect game for the Phils on Father's Day in 1964 against the Mets. Who else does something like that?

Two days later, I learned that Bunning, who would become a congressman and a U.S. senator from Kentucky once his baseball career ended, had passed away at age eighty-five. It's another reminder of a childhood that is slipping away. I remember when none of the players I had pictured on a thin slice of cardboard had departed this life. Now, most players from the 1950s and '60s have been promoted to the eternal diamond.

Fifty years ago, we lived in much simpler times. The fascination of looking at a baseball player's card and then seeing that same player on television gave the baseball card industry instant credibility. THIS player in my six-year-old hand is THAT player on the TV screen—even if the screen transmitted his image in black and white.

Not only are so many players from that era gone—with Jim Bunning among them—but the fascination is also gone from baseball cards. What child could possibly be captivated by a player's face on cardboard in the twenty-first century? Why would they be? It doesn't move. It's not electronic. The game of baseball itself even moves too slowly for most today, and if you are interested, it's far more expedient to pull up the player's image on your iPhone, Android, or tablet.

Jim Bunning was at the end of his Hall of Fame career in 1968 when he joined the Pirates. But he still had time to teach a young pitcher named Steve Blass a little about pitching in the major leagues before hanging up his spikes. Three years later, Blass pitched the Pirates to a World Series victory in Game Seven over the favored Baltimore Orioles.

Bunning wasn't the first baseball card I had. That honor belonged to another Phillies pitcher and another hurler who made his way to Cooperstown—Robin Roberts. It all happened by chance. My sister Chris, who is five years my senior, was on the school bus coming home one day when a classmate dropped a 1960 card of Roberts into the aisle. Chris picked it up and offered it back to a kid named Mark Warner. But Warner said he already had a card of Roberts and that she could go ahead and keep it. She brought it home and showed it to me, we both liked it, and at that moment, we both became interested in collecting more cards. Not only that, but each of us became wildly passionate about the game of baseball. And all because of a duplicate baseball card of Robin Roberts that had harmlessly fallen into the aisle of a school bus one spring afternoon.

The following year, I recall getting at least twenty duplicate cards of Pirates lefty

Harvey Haddix but receiving only one of the Yankees great Mickey Mantle. Some cards were deemed ordinary and others extremely rare. But we valued all of them—everybody from Ron Hansen to Frank Robinson, Bob Buhl to Nolan Ryan.

A good friend of mine asked me recently what I will do with all these baseball cards collected from 1955 through 2010. He suggested I sell them. After all, what happens when I die? Who gets them? His logic made perfect sense.

Trouble is, this isn't a logical decision. It's a part of life and a big chunk of my childhood memories that I would be giving away to someone who will likely not share those memories. By following logic, I'll have a few dollars from selling off Pete Rose, Harmon Killebrew, Roberto Clemente, and Sandy Koufax. But I will no longer own a small fraction of Pete Rose, Harmon Killebrew, Roberto Clemente, or Sandy Koufax. And I will have to live with that.

Equally traumatic would be parting with lesser-known players, such as Don Demeter, Steve Bilko, Chico Cardenas, and Jackie Brandt. I'd have to live with that pain, too.

So, maybe it doesn't make sense to keep all these cards at my age, but not everything in life has to make sense. Sensible or not, I'm not selling.

Speaking of not making sense, Jimmy Piersall certainly didn't. At the first baseball game I ever saw in person, Piersall was playing center field for the Cleveland Indians. When the visiting Baltimore Orioles were at bat and no Orioles' hitter had hit a fly ball in Piersall's direction for several innings, the zany, colorful, and wildly unpredictable Piersall took it upon himself to take a seat on the Cleveland Stadium grass.

That's right—he sat down, legs crossed, in center field. Now, Willie Mays never did that, nor did Omar Moreno or anyone else I saw play. But Piersall did, and he was also an above-average player for the Indians, Red Sox, Senators, Angels, and Mets. His legacy will live on as the only man who ran around the bases after hitting a home run . . . backwards.

I also have his 1960 baseball card. He died two weeks after Bunning passed, at the age of eighty-seven.

You tell me. If you were me, and you had Jimmy Piersall's baseball card, and now knowing what I told you about him, would you sell him off? What price tag would you even attach to his card? The bottom line is this: you can sell something of value and pocket the money it brings.

But ask yourself this question: how do you replace a lost treasure?

A photo of one of my most prized baseball cards: Roberto Clemente, pictured in 1964. (Photo by Charlie Edmisten)

Men in Black

There were two constants in my life growing up: religion and baseball. And many times, the order of their priority got flipped.

Black was always my favorite color, although artists will tell you black is the absence of color. From an early age, I envisioned black as being stately, regal. It signified class with a touch of mystery. While others saw black as the color often worn at funerals, I saw something else. I saw dignity.

Never was this dignity and class more on display than the day I was home sick with my Mom, and two Catholic priests, Father Jimmy Johnson and Father Raymond Ryan, came over to the house to see how I was holding up. Here I was, a seven-year-old kid recovering from either measles or the mumps (I can't remember now which malady left me listless), and these two men emerged from the car and approached the side door. Father Jimmy and Father Raymond were dressed in black from head to toe. Father Jim was holding a card, which was a nice thought. But Father Ray was clutching the most pristine baseball bat I had ever seen.

When I saw them coming, my eyes lit up like it was Christmas Eve. It wasn't. It was June 1961, and the sun was shining.

The bat Father Ray carried looked like it had just come off the assembly line. It was a Louisville Slugger without a single scratch or a dent. It was virgin wood. It resembled the bat Robert Redford made in the baseball film *The Natural* when he carved "Wonderboy" from a tree that had been split by lightning the night before during a heavy thunderstorm.

My mom was as clever as a fox. From the day I was born—July 7, 1954—she sincerely wished I would become a priest. She even went as far as to ask the hospital nurses at Mercy Hospital in Canton, Ohio, where I was born, how the back of my head was shaped. At that time, priests said Mass with their backs to the congregation.

Anyway, Mom knew I loved baseball. I think she put these two men of the cloth up to the task of bringing me a baseball bat to cheer me up. The bat would light up my eyes, and she figured I'd think that if this was something priests did when young boys were taken ill, I'd someday want to become one—a priest, that is, not a ballplayer, nor someone who would write about baseball.

Well, I was indeed impressed. I looked up at those two priests dressed in black and repeatedly thanked them. My mom didn't have to tell me to thank them. I thanked them on my own. At the time, I wondered how they knew this would cheer my spirit. Something tells me my mom had a hand in it.

This was the early 1960s, and the Pittsburgh Pirates were the only other men I recall being dressed in such black, dignified, and stately attire. The Pirates of that era wore sleeveless vests and donned long black sleeves with black caps. The all-black Pirates cap with the gold P remains my favorite. You have to understand that my favorite baseball team wasn't just going to be a team with players I admired. They had to look good, too. I have often felt the same way about women, but that's a discussion for another day.

Dick Schofield, Gene Alley, Bob Veale, Jerry Lynch, Harvey Haddix . . . their baseball cards back then always pictured them wearing the sleeveless look, and in those gray, flannel road uniforms, the black sleeves underneath and the gold trim stood out, especially with the all-black cap with the gold P. This was sartorial splendor at its finest.

Turns out the Pirates really were like Catholic priests, as they moved away from their black, sleeveless look, just as priests don't always wear black anymore. When they do, however, it sends a message that they tend to their flock, and that's a noble and honorable calling.

The Pirates had that same appearance of nobility, so even though it didn't happen this way, they should never have lost a game on Sundays at Forbes Field. Life isn't perfect, but a priest dressed all in black carrying a baseball bat in his hand was darn close to it.

Looking like a priest here. I don't think I'd have made a good one!

A Baseball Lesson in Civil Rights

When I was a kid, civil rights was something you heard about on the nightly news. I'm old enough to remember watching Martin Luther King's march on Selma, Alabama, and when public places had two drinking fountains, one marked for whites and the other for "colored." I remember thinking that we had finally reached equality when President Lyndon Johnson signed the Civil Rights Act of 1964 into law.

Like many people, I separated baseball from the rest of the world. I never thought about whether Bob Gibson and Tim McCarver got along or if there was any racial tension between the two men. Gibson was black, McCarver is white. Both were St. Louis Cardinals, and the pair helped the Redbirds win the 1964 World Series. I had both of their baseball cards, after all, and they both looked happy from what I could see.

I studied civil rights in school, but nobody ever mentioned September 1, 1971. I wonder now why that date was left out of textbooks. Was it because what happened that day had more to do with baseball and not enough about civil rights? That might have been the case in 1971. Not so much today.

It was on that date that the Pittsburgh Pirates fielded the first all-black and Latino lineup in the history of baseball. Quite a milestone considering Jackie Robinson had only broken the game's color barrier less than twenty-five years earlier in 1947. On that night, the Pirates' manager, Danny Murtaugh, turned in a lineup card that included Al "Scoop" Oliver at first base, Rennie Stennett at second base, Jackie Hernandez at shortstop, Dave Cash at third base with Willie Stargell playing left field, Gene Clines patrolling center, and the incomparable Roberto Clemente in right field. Catching was Manny Sanguillen, with pitcher Dock Ellis on the mound.

The landmark occurrence went largely unnoticed by Murtaugh and the players alike until Cash pointed out the obvious to Oliver in the fourth inning. "Hey Scoop!" he cried. "We've got all brothers out here!"

The media missed the milestone as well. There was no coverage of it because there was a strike of all Pittsburgh newspapers at the time. The Pirates defeated the Philadelphia Phillies that night at Three Rivers Stadium 10–7, but that was not the story. The Philadelphia Daily News picked up on it, calling it "Danny Murtaugh's all-soul lineup."

Murtaugh dismissed it, offering his own observation. "When it comes to making out the lineup," said the Bucs' field boss, "I'm colorblind, and my athletes know it. The best men in our organization are the ones who are here. And the ones who are here all play."

September 1, 1971 came to the forefront for me again recently when I read of the passing of Hernandez, the shortstop for the Pirates on that night. Pittsburgh had a great team that year, finishing 97–65, defeating the San Francisco Giants to win the National League pennant, then toppling the heavily favored Baltimore Orioles in the 1971 World Series, four games to three.

Baltimore manager Earl Weaver publicly said the Pirates would never win the Fall Classic with the light-hitting Hernandez playing shortstop. The Cuban-born Hernandez had been a journeyman, marking time in the American League with the Royals, Twins, and Angels before landing in Pittsburgh. Hernandez was stellar, proving Weaver's claim to be false.

Ironically, he recorded the final putout of the seventh game of the Series when he snared a ball hit behind second base. Moving to his left, he fired a bullet to first baseman Bob Robertson to nip the Orioles' Merv Rettenmund for the Series-clinching out.

The Pirates then broke into a frenzied celebration with Hernandez sharing in the glee of the moment. However, years later, Hernandez said it was playing in baseball's first all-black lineup on that September evening that he cherished as his most prized moment in professional baseball.

The event of that night brings to light the line delivered by James Earl Jones in the baseball movie *Field of Dreams*. "You know, we just don't recognize the most significant moments of our lives while they're happening."

Baseball's first all-black and Latino line-up went mostly unnoticed the night it happened in Pittsburgh. But that doesn't mean it should ever be forgotten, overlooked, or uncelebrated going forward.

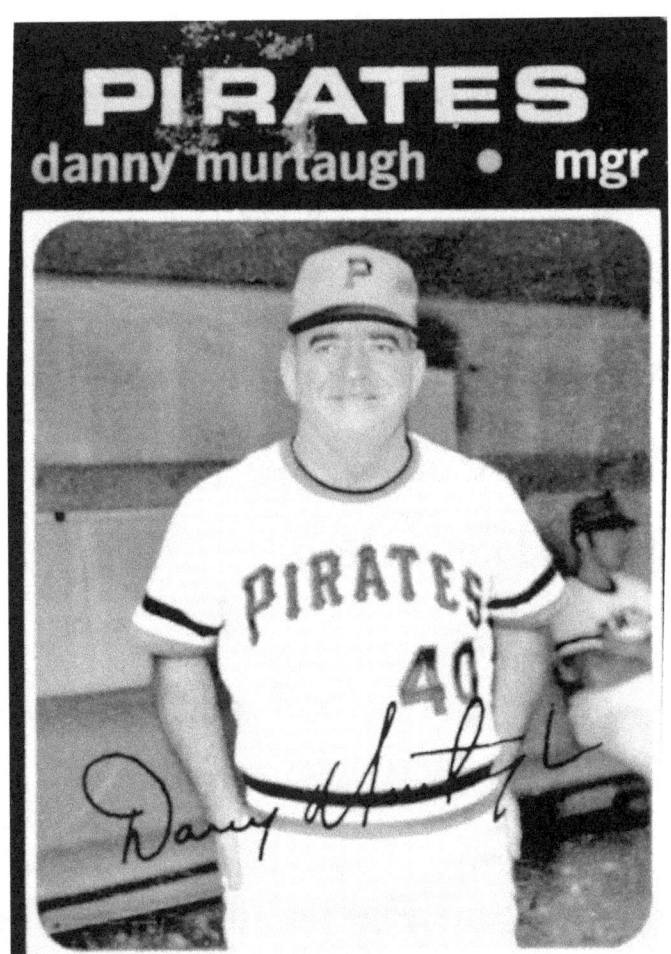

From my personal collection: the 1971 baseball card for Danny Murtaugh, Pirates manager, who fielded the first all-black and Latino lineup. (Photo by Charlie Edmisten)

A Whole New Meaning to Opening Day

As with every other baseball season, I highly anticipated Opening Day of 2018. Opening Day represents a new beginning, another opportunity to erase the past and create a new future of hope and promise. But this year was a little different.

Somehow, this Opening Day had an adverse feel to it, and if you are a fan of the Pittsburgh Pirates, it was easy to figure out why. Within days of each other in December, the Pirates had traded away their best hitter from the previous season and the face of their franchise, Andrew McCutchen, along with pitching staff ace and former number one draft pick Gerrit Cole.

The collection of players coming back in both trades—McCutchen to San Francisco and Cole to Houston—resembled more of what you'd find in your local Walmart bin than any prized possession waiting to be opened on Christmas Eve. One of the players coming back to the Pirates from the Astros in exchange for Cole was rookie third baseman Colin Moran. I didn't know much about this guy, and besides his mother, probably nobody else did either.

But boy, I sure know something about Moran now. He belted a grand slam home run in the Pirates' 5–4 victory in their home opener on April 2 at PNC Park against the Minnesota Twins . . . but I was not there to see it.

I didn't see it on television, hear it broadcast on the radio, or even read about it on my phone. Nothing! What? Did I die? If you know me, you're wondering how it was even possible for me to miss an event such as that. Well, as it turns out, on Monday, April 2, 2018, I was having my very own "opening day" experience—but not in Pittsburgh.

On the previous Friday, I had a heart cath done at Akron's Summa Health Care Center. It revealed the worst possible nightmare, even worse than blowing a three-run lead in the ninth inning: I had multiple blocked arteries, and quadruple heart bypass surgery was immediately necessary. That's equivalent to two strikes and no balls with two men out.

The day I was to be opened up—Opening Day, if you will—happened to be Monday morning, April 2, 2018. My cardiovascular doctor ordered me to take care of this—and to do so right away. He didn't give me an option like, "Go ahead, Ben. Go to Pittsburgh on Monday, watch the home opener, see Moran hit a grand slam, and then when you return, we'll schedule your heart surgery." Uh, NO.

Now, I know what you're thinking. You can always see a ballgame, even a grand slam, on Opening Day, but first, you have to take care of yourself so that you're around for Opening Day next year. Sure, I understand that reasoning. Then again, I discovered that the heart surgeon performing my procedure had successfully performed many of these over his long and distinguished career in medicine. By contrast, how many times will

Moran, or anybody wearing a Pirates' uniform for that matter, swing for the fences and drive in four runs with one level swing before a capacity crowd on Opening Day? I mean, when you look at it that way . . .

The surgery was a complete success, and I read about Moran's accomplishment the next day in the newspaper. Yes, I took care of my health first and foremost. I got the best of both worlds on that Opening Day: I got the chance to still see Moran's grand slam on video once I came home from the hospital, and better yet, I'm still here to relay this story to you.

There are many heartfelt moments in life. I was just lucky enough to experience two in one day . . . on Opening Day, 2018.

By the way, here's a heartwarming update. Andrew "Cutch" McCutchen has signed a one-year deal returning to the Pirates in 2023. Like most fans of the Bucs, my heart skipped a beat too when I heard the news. It will be fun once again to see McCutchen batting in the "heart" of the Pirates' batting order. Welcome home!

This is the hospital where I spent Opening Day, 2018. I went into extra innings before it was over!

Opening Day Heartbreak

Opening Day of a new baseball season has always been a cherished memory of mine, as it has been for many fans. It is a day of rebirth, a fresh slate, a chance to erase the past and begin anew, as it often coincides on the calendar with the Easter season. I haven't seen every Opening Day of my favorite team, the Pittsburgh Pirates, but the years 2018 and 2019 have held unique significance with a dash of irony.

It was Opening Day, April 2, 2018, when the Pirates hosted the Minnesota Twins at PNC Park. I was planning on attending this game, but my plans were suddenly and unexpectedly derailed when I learned I would need four-way heart bypass surgery on—you guessed it—the morning of April 2, 2018.

On Sunday night, the night before my surgery, I was as nervous as an expectant father. What if something went wrong? I had been (sort of) kidding my family and friends that if my surgeon Dr. Baranack's hands slipped halfway through the procedure at Summa Akron City Hospital, I'd end up meeting St. Peter instead of the usher in Section 327 at the ballpark. What would I do then? Ask St. Peter if he gets the MLB channel?

I don't remember much about that long, arduous day. How could I? I was given a local anesthetic and didn't awaken until about seven p.m. that evening, three hours after surgery and long after the Pirates had defeated the Twins 5–4. It wasn't until the following day that I learned that the Pirates had won and that a rookie named Colin Moran was mostly responsible for the victory when he belted a grand slam home run. Darn! I had missed a Pirates' victory (not an everyday practice!) and a grand slam on Opening Day in front of a sellout crowd. Geez, how many times can you expect to witness a feat such as that?

Instead, I had my own Opening Day experience, one I would not wish on anyone. Unless you equate opening your chest as a playing field and four-way bypass representing all four bases on the diamond. But that's a stretch.

In the days and weeks that followed, which then became months, I vowed I would make amends on Opening Day, 2019. The Good Lord was kind enough to see me through to another day, another chance, another game on Opening Day.

A year goes really fast once you get into your sixties. Ever notice that? The next thing I knew, in between getting hammered with Medicare forms and questionnaires, I received an Opening Day postcard from the Pirates in December. "Get your tickets now for Opening Day on Monday, April 1, against the St. Louis Cardinals!" I waited a while, then finally broke down and ordered a ticket online: Row Q in Section 327 for twenty-eight bucks. That included taxes and fees.

The morning of April 1, 2019 was spectacular. Brisk, but spectacular nonetheless. I had taken my daily dosages of medication for controlling blood pressure and cholesterol as prescribed by my cardiologist and was now on the road to Pittsburgh to witness the Opening Day I couldn't see the year before. There was absolutely no way the Pirates were going to lose today. The sun was shining brightly as I watched it ascend over the tree tops on Interstate 76 East. Sometimes, you can feel a victory for your team. If you have a favorite team, you know exactly what I mean.

Once I arrived at my seat, I looked across the PNC Park landscape, and my eyes were locked on the scoreboard's starting lineups. Batting sixth and playing third base for the Pirates was none other than Colin Moran. I immediately imagined Moran hitting yet another grand slam on Opening Day for the second consecutive year. Instead, Moran, making his first start of the season, lashed a first-inning double into the right field corner, plating two runs. It was part of a three-run first inning, and when the dust had settled, the score was Pirates 3, Cardinals 0. How cool is that? The same guy coming up with a big hit again on Opening Day for the Bucs! I was fully conscious for this one. No anesthetic this year!

The Pirates extended their lead to 4–0 behind animated starting pitcher Chris Archer through five innings. This is good, I'm telling myself. But not so fast! St. Louis had a very good team, good enough for some to pick them to reach the World Series. Behind a two-run home run and a bevy of Pirates mistakes that included errors, walks, hit batters, and a base running gaffe, the Cardinals would tie the game in the eighth inning, 4–4.

This was the Lenten season, and I had promised I would give up using foul language. The Pirates' bullpen, however, was apparently also observing Lent, giving up runs.

In the Pirates' half of the eighth, Moran dug into the batter's box. Amidst a sun-baked surface, he swung and lined a bullet to right field. The baseball's trajectory began to rise as it approached the right field wall. Oh, c'mon, man! Moran was not a prodigious power-hitting threat. It was April 1. It had been one year since this guy hit a grand slam on Opening Day that I missed because I was lying unconscious in recovery.

Was this an April Fool's joke? No. It was another home run on Opening Day by Colin Moran! The exit velocity of the ball was 110 miles per hour. It was now Pirates 5, Cardinals 4. Get through one more inning, and the Pirates would have another Opening Day victory with the same guy as the hero. Only this time, I saw it for myself!

However, it's been said that not everything in life will go your way. I know that, but that couldn't apply to this day, could it? Yes, it could. Another error led to the Cardinals scoring the tying run again in the ninth, knotting the score at 5–5. A passed ball in the eleventh inning led to the winning run and a gut-wrenching 6–5 loss to the Cardinals on the day when the Pirates were simply not supposed to lose.

But lose they did. When you're under the knife, you don't feel what is being done to you. When you're awake, you feel everything. The Cardinals cut my heart out on Opening Day, 2019.

On the other hand, you learn to appreciate what you do have. I had a fully functioning heart that year, even if the hated Cardinals stabbed me in it, figuratively speaking. Lord willing, I would get another chance to get the ending I wanted to see once Opening Day, 2020 arrived.

Thank God I'm alive to either rejoice or complain. Life is precious and far more important than winning a baseball game. And yes, that includes winning your home opener.

In baseball, it was just one game, one day. Tomorrow the sun would rise and shine again. And I will once again meet the usher in Section 327. Meeting St. Peter would be nice too . . . but not yet. I'm in no hurry.

Baseball and Race Relations

We have lived so long with racism in the United States that it has become untenable in our words and actions. Unwittingly, it has been handed down through the generations like a rite of passage, often accompanied by ill-suited phrases such as "That's just the way things are."

Like buggy rides in an amusement park, our minds are spinning out of control over racial unrest. Riots and looting in the streets, peaceful (and not so peaceful) protests. A white cop kneeling on the neck of a defenseless black man. Black children shot while sitting in strollers. Minority-owned businessmen and women watching their lives' investments burned to the ground for no reason. Innocent black men gunned down by police during a routine traffic stop, while the next day honorable men and women in blue of any race are shot down in some twisted form of retaliation. The phrase "we've seen it all" certainly seems to apply, doesn't it? If not, we've certainly seen most of it.

Many have no idea what to believe or where to turn. And many would never suspect that in some small way—in a way that they would never have imagined—they just might find solace through the game of baseball.

The initial reaction, of course, is to scoff at the notion that a ball, a leather glove, or a wooden bat could ease the pain of any modern-day social injustice. Those items in and of themselves cannot. However, it isn't what baseball explicitly represents, but its implicit message that we need to retain.

When Thomas Jefferson wrote the Declaration of Independence, he made a provision for baseball, declaring that "all men are free and equal." After all, that's why they are at the ballgame, banker and bricklayer, lawyer and common laborer.

Baseball provided the stage upon which Jackie Robinson crossed the game's color barrier in 1947, playing for the Brooklyn Dodgers. The movie *42*, which celebrates Robinson's life and courageous journey toward equality, portrays that one of the most racist cities Robinson played in was Pittsburgh.

Yet, in a twist of irony, the Pittsburgh Pirates also fielded the first ever all-black starting lineup in baseball twenty-four years later, on September 1, 1971. Danny Murtaugh, the white manager of the Pirates, handed in a lineup card that night with a player of color at each position.

Playing first base was Al Oliver, with Rennie Stennett at second, Jackie Hernandez at shortstop, and Dave Cash manning third base. The outfield, left to right, was patrolled by Willie Stargell, Gene Clines, and Roberto Clemente. Catching that night was Manny Sanguillen, and the starting pitcher was Dock Ellis. Murtaugh wrote out the lineup card not necessarily to help improve race relations in the country, but to give the Pirates the best chance to win the game, which they did, defeating the Philadelphia Phillies that night 10–7.

Larry Doby of the Cleveland Indians followed Robinson to become the first black player in the American League. It was also the Indians who hired the game's first black manager, Frank Robinson, in 1975. Just a year earlier, the nation watched as Hank Aaron of the Atlanta Braves eclipsed the career home run record of the iconic Babe Ruth when he smashed his 715th long ball. A standing ovation followed for Aaron, who had warded off death threats while attempting to overtake the "Sultan of Swat."

This was a cherished record held in high esteem by Ruth, a white man. Yet, as Aaron circled the bases and touched home plate, the capacity crowd that night in Atlanta—both black and white patrons—stood in unison, applauding a black man in the Deep South.

Maybe these events in and of themselves will never solve or even ease the strain of division in our country. But we all could still keep them in mind. We could recognize that we all need a break from the chaos, unrest, and injustice.

Maybe if we made ourselves aware of how baseball has connected lives and generations in the past, bridged the racial divide, and brought us all together, even for a short time, it just might help heal so many open wounds in a way that few other activities can.

Maybe we could one day realize that the answers we are looking for to connect the brotherhood of man will never come from the news media, the White House, or the statehouse.

Maybe it will finally occur to us that the answers we seek can only be found within ourselves, and that baseball can serve as our collective catharsis to bring us the peace and harmony that we all seek and so richly deserve.

Lost Ticket

It still felt like summer when I walked to the mailbox, opened the door, and saw an envelope that made me think it was Christmas even though it was mid-September.

I slit open the top of the envelope, blew into it, and reached in. When my hand pulled out what lay inside, I soon realized it really was Christmas Day. It was a ticket.

No, not a ticket to the Ed McMahon sweepstakes. Not a ticket from the Akron Police Department for doing thirty-two in a twenty-five. And not a ticket to a local restaurant where they feed you a steak dinner only to bore you to tears soon afterward when some financial analyst guru tells you how you need to save for retirement now because Social Security will be abolished by 2030.

No, this was a ticket to something with much greater meaning and value: Game One of the 1992 World Series, the Pittsburgh Pirates against the Toronto Blue Jays.

If you are not a baseball fan, think about this logically. If this were a ticket to listen to some guy pontificate over how to save for your kids' college, how appealing of a conversation would that be in eighteen years? Maybe he doesn't want to go to college, or she has a scholarship and thus doesn't need what you saved.

But if you can tell your kids and grandkids about attending the first game of the 1992 World Series, they'll ask you about that. That's intriguing. Who pitched? Who won? What was the crowd like on that Saturday night in October at the now-demolished Three Rivers Stadium? Did you get any autographs? Did you keep your scorecard as a memento from the occasion?

The point is, you get to converse around the dinner table or at your neighborhood tavern about being at a World Series game with a large group of people who have never experienced being at such an event and are now asking you what it was like. Do you really think large groups of people will ask you what it was like to listen to a financial analyst after a steak dinner?

Okay, so maybe a winning lottery ticket would top a ticket to the first game of the 1992 World Series. But seeing your favorite team play in the World Series is far more likely than winning a million dollars, right? (If you're a fan of the Cleveland Guardians, you may want to refrain from answering that question!)

The World Series ticket was now in my hand. One ticket. One seat, located in row three down the right field line at Three Rivers Stadium. Field level. Eye level. Game time: 8:20 p.m. to accommodate television.

Only, the game was never played.

Thirty years later, I'm still wondering how and why. The answer comes down to one person: Sid Bream. Or maybe two people: Sid Bream and Barry Bonds.

The Blue Jays were already in the World Series representing the American League that year. They now awaited their opponent, either the Pirates or the Atlanta Braves. As a Pirates' season ticket holder, I was one of the chosen loyal fans the club contacted well in advance of the World Series in October by sending out tickets in September. Teams can't wait until the last minute to get those in the mail. The Pirates were playing the Braves in the National League Championship Series in the seventh and deciding game. The Pirates led 2–0 heading into the bottom of the ninth inning at Atlanta's Fulton County Stadium, also since leveled into oblivion. (Thank God!)

So, the Bucs had a 2–0 advantage, and their best pitcher, Doug Drabek, was on the mound. Drabek was a former twenty-game winner who had won baseball's most prestigious pitching award: the Cy Young Award, symbolic of the league's best hurler.

The Braves hadn't done much against him in eight innings. We had Drabek on the mound and a strong bullpen behind him, just in case Drabek faltered. As the last of the ninth was about to commence, I told my wife at the time, "We got this! We'll beat Atlanta and go on to play Toronto Saturday night in Pittsburgh."

Wow! The first time I would ever witness a World Series game! It was three nights away and more importantly, three outs away. Dust off that seat in row three down the right field line, I'm thinking to myself. I'm going to the World Series, and tonight before I go to bed, I will lay out my favorite black and gold Pirates outfit that I'll wear to the game days in advance. I couldn't wait. It really was an early Christmas.

But oh yes, that ninth inning . . .

The first batter to face Drabek doubled into the right field corner. The next batter reached on an error by our sure-handed second baseman, Jose Lind. The next batter was Bream, a former Pirate who signed as a free agent with Atlanta. Bream, a Pittsburgh native, walked, and suddenly, the bases were loaded with Braves and nobody out.

Pirates Manager Jim Leyland emerged from the dugout and removed Drabek from the game. In came our best reliever, Stan Belinda. At this point, I was still confident. Belinda had saved thirty games during the season, and his right-handed "buggy-whip" motion made it difficult for the hitter to pick up the baseball as it was released from his hand.

Atlanta's Ron Gant, however, had no such difficulty. He hammered a Belinda offering very deep to left field. *Oh my God, we lost,* I thought. It's going to be a grand slam home run. My heart was in my esophagus. But no! Bonds reached up at the last minute with his large mitt and safely corralled the baseball in front of the wall. Whew! The runner at third tagged up and scored, while the runners at first and second tagged up and advanced to second and third base. It was now Pirates 2, Braves 1 with one out.

After another walk reloaded the bases, Belinda bore down and induced the next Braves hitter to pop out to Lind at second base. Two outs! One more out, and I'm going to the World Series!

Atlanta then pinch-hit this guy who frankly wasn't very good. I was stunned. I don't know why the Braves would send this guy up to hit, but I reasoned that was fine with me. This player had spent most of the season in the minor leagues and was not that good of a hitter. His name was Francisco Cabrera.

Belinda missed the strike zone with his first two pitches. The next pitch was smoked by Cabrera to left field but was foul by a significant measure. The count was two balls and one strike. At this point, Pirates' centerfielder Andy Van Slyke motioned to Bonds, who was playing back in left field, to come in. Years later, Van Slyke explained that Cabrera was a light-hitting outfielder. He knew if he hit it at all, he would pull it and it would be to left field, but not that deep because Cabrera lacked power.

He also knew that Bream was the runner on second, and if you knew anything about Sid Bream—and the Pirates did—you knew he was so slow afoot that he couldn't beat a pregnant turtle in a forty-yard dash. But when Van Slyke motioned to Bonds to come in a few steps, Bonds responded by giving Van Slyke the international peace symbol. Bonds remained stationary in deep left field.

Belinda's 2–1 pitch was high and over the outside edge of the plate. Cabrera extended his bat across the plate and executed a whirlwind-type swing. The ball was hit squarely on a line drive, past the shortstop position, and, sure enough, into left field toward a charging Bonds. The runner on third base scored easily, tying the game at 2–2. Bonds circled in behind the ball and now had farther to run in to field it, having spurned Van Slyke's suggestion just one pitch earlier to move in closer toward the infield. Meanwhile, Bream had taken off from second base and was churning with all the swiftness of a John Deere tractor mowing an Iowa hayfield.

When Bream rounded third base and headed for home plate, Bonds was fielding the ball in left. If he'd had a shorter distance to run, of course, the ball would already have been released from Bonds's hand in left field, and its trajectory would be well on its way to Pirates catcher Mike LaValliere. As it was, Bream, easily the slowest man in baseball, now actually had a chance to score the winning run.

As Bream, the former Pirate who lived in a Pittsburgh suburb, began to go into his slide, LaValliere had to reach toward the first base side of home plate to receive the ball, which he did deftly. However, LaValliere then had to extend back across the plate to tag Bream out. LaValliere reached valiantly while Bream's left toe stretched toward the plate. The tag was made on Bream's left thigh. The suspense reached its zenith, and without hesitation, the umpire announced his verdict...

"Safe!"

The television camera was shaking. Fulton County Stadium erupted into pure bedlam. Bream was smothered under a pile of celebrating Braves at home plate as a deafening roar blanketed all of Georgia. Final score: Braves 3, Pirates 2. It would be the Braves, not my beloved Pirates, going on to the World Series on Saturday. Hurriedly, CBS Sports officials had to move the celebratory champagne bottles from the Pittsburgh clubhouse to the Atlanta clubhouse. Emotions switched ever so swiftly and unexpectedly.

My face was flushed as I tossed aside my scorecard. I was on my knees in our Akron apartment, pounding the carpeted floor in utter disdain and disbelief. "No, no, no," I cried. "*Nooooooooooooo!*"

Real tears streamed down my face. The pain left a feeling of hollowness similar to losing something or someone close to you. To many, that sounds silly. But not to any true baseball fan who passionately follows and supports his team.

That game was played thirty years ago. Much has changed since that fateful night in Atlanta on Wednesday, October 14, 1992.

The Braves? They would lose the 1992 World Series in six games to the Blue Jays. They would beat the Indians three years later in the 1995 Fall Classic. The Braves won another World Series crown in 2021.

The Pirates? This game remains the most excruciating defeat in the one-hundred-and-thirty-five-year history of the franchise. The Pirates would go on to suffer twenty straight losing seasons from 1993 through 2012, a North American record for futility by any professional team in any sport.

While the Pirates qualified for the playoffs three straight years from 2013 through 2015, they are now considered one of baseball's five worst teams.

Doug Drabek? He is now retired from pro-baseball and lives in Texas. His son reached the Major Leagues as a pitcher.

Andy Van Slyke? He became a first base coach for the Detroit Tigers, who, unlike Bonds, obeyed his commands. His son, Scott, was an outfielder for the Los Angeles Dodgers.

Stan Belinda? He lives in relative obscurity in upstate Pennsylvania. For the first several years after the loss in Atlanta, he received death threats in the mail. He was nicknamed "The Piano Man" because it must have felt to Belinda that he was carrying the weight of a piano on his shoulders. I sincerely hope he has let it go.

Francisco Cabrera? He was out of baseball less than two years after the biggest hit of his career. He never became a starting player in the major leagues, let alone a star. The only time he sees a big-league diamond now is if the Braves ask him back to throw out a ceremonial first pitch.

Sid Bream? Here's a touch of irony. Several years ago, I was standing behind the batting cage at the Pirates' spring training home in Bradenton, Florida. A lanky left-handed hitting coach was slapping ground balls to the Pirates infielders during a morning practice. As the coach turned around, his sturdy, rugged, suntanned face came into view. It was Sid Bream.

For many years after that game, Bream hit the "rubber chicken" circuit in and around Pittsburgh, where he was a motivational speaker. There were times he was robustly booed. Today, as a baseball fan, Bream roots for the Pirates.

Barry Bonds? It is Bonds—more so than Belinda or Bream—who is widely regarded as the villain of this terrible result in Pirates history. What if Bonds, a surly, boorish, self-centered, arrogant, yet tremendous baseball player, had heeded Van Slyke's advice? Surely, he would have thrown out Bream at home plate that night. "The Night Sid Slid" would never have lived in Atlanta's baseball folklore. Worse yet for Bonds, he would become nearly everyone's villain. The man who has hit more home runs than any player in baseball history—762—is still not in the Hall of Fame because of his rampant use of steroids. He may never enter the game's immortal shrine because of it. Even if he does reach the Hall of Fame, in Pittsburgh and elsewhere, he will always be remembered for not being able to throw out the slowest man in baseball when it mattered most.

And me? Oh, I'm okay. I haven't pounded a floor since that awful night. I no longer purchase season tickets, although I do attend many baseball games. Less than a week after that game, I mailed my foiled World Series ticket back to Pittsburgh. I'm sure it is destroyed by now. But many baseball collectors would argue that it has unique value: a ticket to a World Series game that was never played. Once a prized possession taken from my mailbox on a sunny September day, it was thought to be a ticket that would spin the turnstiles at Three Rivers Stadium, allowing me to witness the climax of a baseball season. Instead, it exists as an invitation to a dark, cruel memory. It is an imaginary key that will never open a door. And the lost ticket will only be killed once the Pirates reach the World Series again.

In the meantime, I suppose I can purchase a ticket to a potentially far less gut-wrenching event . . . like listening to some financial analyst after dinner at a local restaurant. Time to go now, here comes my waiter. I think I'll have a steak, well done.

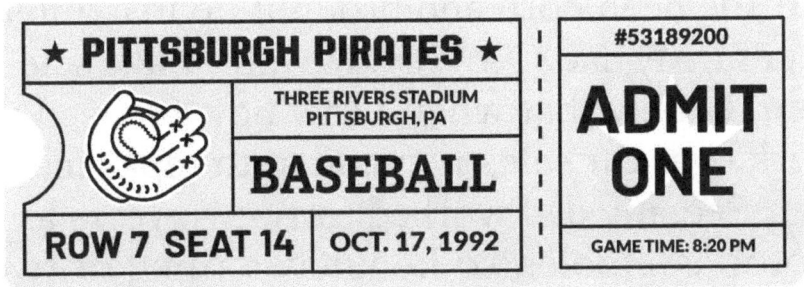

(Graphic by Ryan Humbert)

Practically at Forbes

Sales is one of the most challenging of professions, I'm told. I guess I should have realized that during the 1960s. My mom would have been a great salesperson had she been born and brought up in a different era. My dad? No way! He didn't like salesmen. I knew that when I saw how he used to work over car salesmen and auto repairmen.

See, my dad worked forty-two years as a motor assembler, so he knew a thing or two about cars. He knew if some mechanic was trying to talk him into needing a part or a service that wasn't necessary. And he knew how to defuse a car salesman's ploy to add on a bell or whistle that he didn't actually need.

But being the most practical man who ever lived, he also taught me how necessary it was to have other perks, such as a rear window defogger or undercoating, given the extreme Ohio weather conditions. Practicality ruled Dad's every decision. If he didn't need to do it, he simply didn't do it. If he didn't need to spend more, he didn't spend it. And despite my urging him to take me to Forbes Field to see a Pittsburgh Pirates baseball game, he saw no reason to do so, especially since it was closer for him to drive the family to Cleveland to see an Indians game.

Of course, like everyone else in my family, Dad was not a Pirates fan in the first place, so who cared about seeing them? Well, I did, but that wasn't practical thinking.

The practical thing was driving to Cleveland, which was an hour or so closer than Pittsburgh. After all, Pittsburgh wasn't even in Ohio. Heck, back in those days before highways and interstates were fully built, driving to Pittsburgh was a full day's journey, one that required bringing a packed lunch.

It made sense . . . from a practical standpoint, anyway. Dad reasoned that we had major league baseball much closer to home than driving to Pittsburgh, and we'd save on gas and wear and tear on the car by going to a game in Cleveland. The Indians were the hometown team we grew up watching, and Dad was an Indians fan through and through. Besides, Dad needed a roadmap to find Forbes Field in Pittsburgh. He didn't know anyone who had ever been there. Neither did I, but I still wanted to go.

Fortunately, being the most practical man ever, Dad was a member of the Ohio AAA Auto Club. He urged all of us (especially me) to join once we were of legal driving age. What happens if you break down on the highway and you don't have any insurance? Boy, am I glad I joined! I've lost count of how many times I've stalled, broke down, or been stuck with a car that wouldn't turn over since I joined the AAA in 1974 at age twenty.

In those days, GPS hadn't even been thought of, so you had to see a travel-by-car representative at the local AAA office if you wanted to go anywhere. She would use a yellow magic marker to draw what was known as a Trip-Tik, which indicated your starting point and final destination. Membership had its privileges! The turnpike wasn't fully developed to drive from Canton to Pittsburgh, so you had to travel on Route 30 eastbound. Now, Route 30 was reliable, but also long, winding through the hills and various towns of eastern Ohio and western Pennsylvania. Dad was leery about breaking down or getting lost just to see a ballgame in the next state that could be more expediently accomplished by simply driving north for one hour to Cleveland. It was infinitely more practical to travel a road he knew very well to see a team he found far more appealing.

He thought I should see it the same way. But I was a kid and practical myself—I knew Forbes was on its last legs. A new stadium beckoned on the city's North Side, and I wanted to see the historic Forbes before it met with the wrecking ball.

The tipping point in my favor came during the summer of 1969. Remember, religion and baseball were two major influences in my young life. Little did I know it would be a religious person who would ultimately pave my road to Forbes Field. Sister Genevieve Burke was a close friend of my mom's, and that summer, Sister Jenny was being sent to the Towers in Oakland near Forbes Field to assist the Diocese of Pittsburgh in a religious education program.

At last, I had a reason, a blue-chip, if you will, to get Dad and the rest of the family to venture over to Pittsburgh to see a Pirates game. And without Sister Jenny being stationed in Pittsburgh that summer, it would never have happened.

Now, there was no way we would attend a night game. Dad wasn't about to attempt to find an unfamiliar place at night. But a day game seemed plausible. And there were always Sunday afternoon games. We could now drive over and visit Sister Jenny at The Towers, and since it was close—especially since it was close—we could then walk over to Forbes Field on August 3, 1969 to watch the Pirates play the San Francisco Giants.

My mom and Sister Jenny talked to each other the entire time. My dad looked bored, and my sister Chris sat wondering what the Indians' score was that Sunday afternoon. Forbes Field was falling apart by 1969, but since I'd never been there before, it looked majestic to me. A year later, the Pirates were playing in Three Rivers Stadium. But not on Sunday, August 3, 1969. It didn't seem like a big deal at the time, but we were watching a half dozen future Hall of Famers that day—Willie McCovey, Willie Mays, and starting pitcher Gaylord Perry for the Giants; and Roberto Clemente, Willie Stargell, and Bill Mazeroski for the hometown Pirates.

Clemente connected for an opposite field home run off of Perry in the eighth inning, slicing the Giants' lead to 3–2. But the Bucs couldn't complete the comeback. I remember feeling empty and foolish. I had wanted to see a Pirates home game for years, and when we finally saw them, they lost. I did come home with a gold Pirates pennant that day, and we watched as Perry signed post-game autographs for fans outside the ballpark. There was virtually no security around him. Before the game, I got two Pirate signatures, one from third baseman Jose Pagan and another from outfielder Carl Taylor.

It was a much simpler time, no doubt. Despite my disappointment in the outcome, I vowed I'd get back to Forbes.

And I did—just nineteen days later . . .

Sister Jenny, who made my first trip to Forbes Field possible.

Hot August Night

Over fifty years ago, a high school buddy of mine invited me to join him and his dad to attend a twi-night doubleheader at Forbes Field. Owen Riley and his dad were both originally from McKeesport, Pennsylvania, a community in suburban Pittsburgh. The plan was to attend the two games and then have dinner and spend the night at Owen's grandmother's house.

It was August 22, 1969, and for me, it was like a summer vacation. It turned out even better than that, as the Pirates swept the twin bill 8-2 and 5-3 over the Cincinnati Reds. We got a chance to see the great Roberto Clemente play right field from our seats, which were within close proximity down the first base line.

I remember telling Owen how surreal it would be to also see Bill Mazeroski, the Pirates' second baseman, win one of the two games by hitting a walk-off home run. Many baseball fans and historians vividly recall the home run struck by "Maz" at that same ballpark just nine years earlier that had given the Pirates a clinching seventh-game World Series victory over the New York Yankees.

Lo and behold, on this night, the Pittsburgh club did win the second game with a walk-off home run—although it wasn't off Mazeroski's bat. Portsmouth, Ohio native Al Oliver instead struck the winning home run. I can still see Oliver rounding third base, and in those bygone days, fans spilled out onto the field to congratulate him, in much the same manner Mazeroski was greeted by fans in October 1960 after his historic blast cleared the Forbes Field wall in left. Do that deed today, and the police will handcuff you.

Maybe the stakes weren't as high this time given the fact this was merely a regular season game in the heat of August. Indeed, it was a "Hot August Night" that occurred long before Neil Diamond coined the same phrase on one of his greatest hits albums. This home run, however, stuck with me more, as I was there to witness it.

The Pirates were in third place at the time, trailing the first-place Chicago Cubs by eight games. Second place belonged to the New York Mets, who would eventually take over the National League East lead during the Cubs' epic collapse in '69, the year the Miracle Mets would eventually win the World Series.

This wasn't the Pirates' year, but you could see what they had coming. Their farm system was brimming with talent, producing not only Oliver, but other young, impactful stars such as Manny Sanguillen, Dave Cash, Richie Hebner, Fred Patek, and Bob Robertson. Combining those promising young players with the likes of Clemente, Mazeroski, and Willie Stargell fueled the Pirates' own World Series triumph over the favored Baltimore Orioles just two years later in 1971.

I couldn't sleep that night at Owen's grandmother's, partly because of reliving Oliver's winning home run and partly because of the sound of a train that rolled through McKeesport. The flashing red lights reflected on the ceiling above my bed in the guest room. I was fifteen and hadn't really been away from home before then. The experience made such an impression at the time that I wrote about it the next day in a letter home to my family, which seems laughable now, especially since the letter I mailed back to Ohio would beat me home by a few hours a couple of days later. The post office was swifter back then, I guess.

It's funny what sticks with you. Incidental experiences of my youth seem to grow more significant with the passage of time. I'm not sure if I can even tell many people about August 22, 1969 today. The response from many would be, "Yeah, so what?" But the experience of being away from home like that, not being with my parents, and of course with baseball as the centerpiece of my sojourn made it oh so impressionable for a late 1960s teenager.

Not only is that type of experience likely lost on today's youth, but sadly, Forbes Field no longer stands, and neither do twi-night doubleheaders. Owen's dad and grandmother have passed away, and I haven't seen my high school friend in years. Like so many things from a half-century ago, events become frozen in time. But it's never a bad idea to resurrect them and relive a moment that makes me smile.

Bradenton-Sarasota Calling!

Like clockwork, it happens every year, right after the Super Bowl. Once the big game is over and the pizzas and Doritos have been consumed, it's time to move on to what's next. Now, that could be many things to many different people, of course. But for me, it can only mean one thing.

It's not like I've done this every year like some rite of passage. But that doesn't mean the Gulf Island beaches on Florida's west coast don't come calling. They do.

The first time I visited Bradenton-Sarasota was in 1997 as an anniversary celebration with my wife at the time. We returned four years later in 2001. I didn't make it back down until seven years after that, this time by myself, in 2008. I went again in 2011, then had another gap, not revisiting to hear the waves until 2017. I then went back each of the next two years, but I didn't return in 2020 because . . . well, we all know why.

The itch is back to once again visit the beaches of Anna Maria Island, Bradenton, Holmes Beach, Coquina Beach, and Longboat Key. If you've been there, you know exactly what I mean. If you haven't, go while you can. You won't regret it. The sunsets on Anna Maria Island are like something out of a Robert Frost poem. The potent and powerful Gulf waves pound the rocks, spread through the sugar-like sand, and then rescind back. The soft island breeze that gently separates your hair strands brings you to the quick realization that you're not in Kansas anymore.

Now what, pray tell, does any of this have to do with baseball? If you know me, you know that no matter the subject matter or circumstance, I will find some way, some meandering of my thought pattern, to connect whatever the subject may be back to the national pastime. Well, as it turns out, Bradenton has been the spring training home of the Pittsburgh Pirates since 1969. So, not only can you enjoy an orange swirl ice cream cone at the Mixon Fruit Farms, just down the road from Pirate City, the team's training facility, but you can also partake of Mexican fare at the Wicked Cantina or enjoy grouper at The Beachhouse, my first stop once I land and get settled.

Incidentally, I never had an ice cream cone in March until I visited Bradenton. Have you? The orange and grapefruit juice at Mixon's is also spectacular, and they even allow you free samples.

I don't want to turn this into a Chamber of Commerce brochure, but you get the idea. The world in cold, wintry Ohio and Pennsylvania is lackluster on, say, March 26. But in Bradenton, it can be seventy-five degrees, with the sun shining brightly against a clear blue sky. In that kind of setting, the crack of the bat against a baseball is the best sound you could hear, save for the first cry of your first-born child.

Baseball can lead us into so many uncharted waters. For instance, I've known for over fifty years that Bradenton was the Pirates' spring home. I knew the team trained there. I knew everyone from Roberto Clemente to Richie Hebner to Andrew McCutchen and now Ke'Bryan Hayes has stepped into the batting cage on one of its many ballfields. But until I actually visited, I didn't know there was white sand on Gulf Drive outside Sharky's Restaurant, where you can order actual shark off the menu.

I didn't know there was a guy strumming a guitar at the Wicked Cantina and singing "Sundown" by Gordon Lightfoot. I didn't know about the chocolate cake and coffee you could order at Euphemia Haye upstairs in the restaurant's Hay Loft in Longboat Key. Heck, I didn't even know how tan I could get from lying in the sand at Coquina Beach with not a care in the world or a single thought about my job back home that would be there to greet me once I returned from paradise.

Is this beginning to sound like another Chamber of Commerce brochure? Sorry.

We've all heard ballplayers say, "I owe it all to baseball." They'll tell you how the game has influenced their lives or even saved them from a deviant path that could have led to a destructive life of poverty, crime, or isolation. Maybe that wouldn't have happened to me. But certainly, because of baseball, I've uncovered so many other experiences unrelated to the game but realized just the same. My initial intention was to travel south to experience spring training baseball and the Pirates' spring home, but so many other experiences walked into my life that I could never have expected. And isn't that the case with so many parts of life? While we turn the handle on one door, another magically swings open.

Well, I've got to run. Time to pack the suntan lotion and wear sandals for a week. If you can't make it down, I'll understand. I'll be sure to bring you back a t-shirt—and a travel brochure!

Photos of me and the Gulf. My first stop is always The Beachhouse, where I enjoy a drink with an umbrella in it!

Rennie Stennett

I remember the day Rennie Stennett got the call. The Pittsburgh Pirates had their new second baseman of the future. Here he was, a twenty-year-old phenom coming up to the big leagues to play a position that, for the Pirates, was already one of both grace and greatness.

Dave Cash manned second base for Pittsburgh when the Bucs won the World Series over Baltimore in seven games in 1971. When the Pirates won the 1960 Series, it was another second baseman who clubbed a historic and iconic home run to defeat the favored New York Yankees in seven games. Rennie Stennett was never going to equal what Bill Mazeroski did on October 13, 1960. Some weren't sure if he was even Cash's equivalent.

But Stennett did something in baseball that no man had ever done before or since. I listened on my mom's Magnavox radio the day he sprayed seven base hits through the blades of grass in seven at-bats in a 22–0 demolition of the Chicago Cubs at Wrigley Field. Four singles, two doubles, and one triple on September 16, 1975.

Like Maz's home run in 1960, Stennett's display seems to grow in greatness over time. Upon his death in May 2021 at age seventy-two, the accomplishment took on even greater significance. He came to be known as "Mr. 7-for-7."

Once a player passes on, his records and his very being seem to grow in scope. Ever notice that? Too bad it takes losing someone to remind us of what that person once accomplished. What joy he brought to our youth. What impact he made on his teammates, the game of baseball, and us as kids. As noted earlier, Stennett's name also was penciled into the lineup by Manager Danny Murtaugh to play second base on September 1, 1971, that historic night when Pittsburgh fielded the first-ever all-black and Latino starting nine in baseball history.

Cash was eventually traded to Philadelphia for pitching help in the form of lefthander Ken Brett. The Pirates also had another great second baseman in their system at the time, Willie Randolph. He, too, was dealt away to the Yankees, where he became a fixture on many of the Bombers' championship teams in the 1970s. Maz? He retired and did a lot of banquet speeches about what it was like to hit the home run that won a World Series.

But nobody else who played second base for the Pirates—not Cash, Maz, Randolph, Johnny Ray, Jose Lind, Carlos Garcia, Freddie Sanchez, Josh Harrison, or Adam Frazier—ever slashed seven base hits in seven plate appearances in a single game. And those are a lot of high-quality second basemen!

We're reminded that we should all take note and enjoy true greatness as it unfolds before us. It is quite likely that we will never see something like it ever again in our lifetime.

The Phone Call

When you reach a certain age, you get scared when the phone rings. Will the caller be a relative telling you your grandmother, grandfather, parent, or sibling has passed away? Will it be someone in law enforcement breaking the news about an accident on the interstate involving a loved one?

However, you don't scare easily when the phone rings when you're eighteen. Not until January 1, 1973.

It was already a sad day. Mom had ordered us kids to start taking down the Christmas decorations. I always wanted to keep them up until mid-February, but Mom was done with the live pine tree by New Year's Eve and was starting to forget how she had arranged her Victorian furniture since Dad had hauled the tree in more than two weeks ago.

The phone was on a wall in the kitchen, where I happened to be while the others were taking down bows and pine cones in the living room. The phone rang, and I answered. Probably one of my Mom's friends calling to ask her about a church bake sale, I thought, or maybe one of my sister's friends. It turned out it was one of my friends, Louie Eberhart.

Louie had been a good friend since our grade school days. He was a Yankees fan, and I, of course, liked the Pirates. I used to take baseball cards of Yankees I got to show him at school during recess—Dooley Womack, Hal Reniff, Tom Tresh.

"Hey Ben, it's Lou," he said.

"Hi, Lou! How was your Christmas?"

"Great," he replied. "Listen, I've got some bad news. Roberto Clemente was killed in a plane crash last night."

"Ha ha, good one, Lou. You're just jealous because the Pirates won the World Series last year, and the Yankees weren't even there!"

The Pirates had defeated the Orioles in seven games to win the Series in 1971. Clemente hit .414 and was named the Series Most Valuable Player. But now, the only thing that became more silent than Baltimore's bats in that series was this phone conversation. Dead silence on the line.

"C'mon, Lou," I finally managed. "Clemente died in a plane crash? Why would he be flying a plane?"

Of course, my friend went on to explain that the great Pirates right fielder had boarded an overloaded aircraft that should never have taken off in an effort to save earthquake-ravaged victims in Nicaragua. The longer the conversation went on, the more it started sinking in. I began to realize that Lou wasn't kidding about this. Remember, in the early 1970s, there was no Internet, no ESPN, no cable, no iPhones. Either you got your news from Walter Cronkite, or Louie Eberhart called you and told you what happened.

I soon went into a daze. How could Roberto Clemente, my favorite baseball player on my favorite team, be dead at age thirty-eight? How could someone like that, in the prime of life, who still looked like he could have played for five more seasons with the shape he was in, suddenly be gone forever?

I can't say this was more tragic news than the deaths of John F. Kennedy or Martin Luther King. Those men were leaders of our country. Roberto wasn't even an American. But Kennedy's and King's deaths were about politics and racial injustice and the CIA and probably the Mob. So while tragic, in retrospect they seemed less surprising to me. After all, there's always some crackpot taking a shot at a famous political or religious figure.

But Clemente? I saw him play in person! I saw him hit a walk-off home run in July, 1972 off Ferguson Jenkins that beat the Chicago Cubs 4–3 at Three Rivers Stadium. I had a number of his baseball cards. Kennedy and King I only saw on television.

Clemente was a magnificently talented athlete who could belt line drives over second base on a pitch low and outside the strike zone. A human gazelle as he galloped the base paths. A right arm that resembled a bazooka. A man of boundless pride and energy. A leader both as a ballplayer and as a man of conscience and selflessness. Number Twenty-One of the Pittsburgh Pirates.

The Roberto Clemente statue stands proudly outside PNC Park. (Photo courtesy Life Journeys/Alamy Stock Photos)

Even today, five decades after his untimely death, Clemente's passing is surreal.

There is no other decorated athlete before or since whose memory has been kept alive more than Clemente. The outfield wall in right field at PNC Park today stands twenty-one feet high, the number on his jersey. Thousands of children not even born when he played or when he perished on December 31, 1972 have worn that jersey. The Sixth Street bridge that feeds directly into PNC Park was renamed the Roberto Clemente Bridge when the new ballpark in Pittsburgh opened in 2001. Countless schools, libraries, and hospitals worldwide have been renamed in his honor.

Every year, Major League Baseball honors a player from each of the thirty teams as a recipient of the Roberto Clemente Award, given to the player who best exemplifies greatness and humanitarianism on and off the field. Roberto's widow, Vera, and her sons have founded Ciudad de Portiva, a sports city in Clemente's native San Juan, Puerto Rico, which encourages young athletes to participate in sports and exercise and develop their minds, bodies, and spirits for competition.

Clemente sacrificed his life for the good of his fellow man by boarding that plane and attempting to aid those far less fortunate than he. I remember the Pirates' public relations spokesperson, Sally O'Leary, saying that in the days and weeks that followed, fans would call in to donate $21.21 to help fund the Clemente statue that was unveiled outside Three Rivers Stadium on July 8, 1994. I attended the event on my fortieth birthday. I had donated my $21.21 to help make the statue a reality.

All that, including another Pirates' World Series championship in 1979, would happen after that fateful phone call on New Year's Day, 1973. But all I knew when I picked up the phone that day and talked to my friend Louie was that what had happened seemed like an unfathomable, cruel joke. I remember my parents saying I was walking around like a zombie, trying to somehow grasp the gravity of the situation.

It didn't affect anyone else in my family like it did me. They were saddened, to be sure, but the Pirates were not my family's favorite team, and Clemente, despite his greatness, was not their favorite player. For me, it was a life-changing moment. I realized then that even the most physically gifted among us could be taken. Even someone as strong, healthy, and vibrant as Clemente can have his life abruptly ended.

But Roberto Clemente's spirit has never been silenced. My recollection of him playing right field at Forbes Field and later Three Rivers Stadium will never wane. I have pictures all over my man cave today of the man known as "The Great One." And just like the twenty-one-foot-high wall at PNC Park, those images, unlike the Christmas decorations on the day of that fateful phone call, will never come down.

The Coronavirus Curveball

If April 1 is known as April Fool's Day, the time has come for April 2 to have a name and an identity all its own. Two years ago, on April 2, 2018, I had to miss the Pittsburgh Pirates' home opener against the Minnesota Twins at PNC Park because I underwent four-way heart bypass surgery.

The Pirates won that game, 5–4, thanks to a grand slam home run off the bat of third baseman Colin Moran. And I missed the whole thing.

I didn't awake in recovery until seven that evening and had no idea what had happened until the next day. The next day! We live in a world of immediacy, and I didn't know the Pirates won until the next freaking day!

So here we are, two years later, on April 2, 2020. I had already arranged to purchase a ticket to the Pirates' home opener, this time against the Cincinnati Reds. April 2 fell on a Thursday. No problem getting off work—my schedule in advertising sales is as flexible as a Jane Fonda workout routine. The Pirates told me by e-mail in February that the ticket for April 2 against the Reds would be mailed out the first week or two in March. Okay. Sounds good, or so I thought.

But then we all know what happened in March. Out of left field, or more specifically, out of China, came the Coronavirus Curveball.

The curveball is often hard to hit because you don't know which way it's going to break. That's how this worldwide pandemic is, too. Because of the outbreak, Major League Baseball, in step with all other professional and amateur sports and the Olympic Games, postponed the start of the season. No game on April 2. The home opener was scratched.

It's brutally ironic. Now that I have a

fully functioning heart and don't have to deal with a knife, I must deal with a virus, just like everyone else, baseball fan or not.

Strange day, April 2.

We are instructed nationally to practice social distancing, keeping ourselves six feet apart from others at all times. Baseball practically invented the concept of social distancing, so I'm pretty familiar with it. Six feet? Heck, it's sixty feet and six inches from the pitcher's mound to the batter. It's ninety feet from home plate to first base, another ninety feet from first base to second, and ninety more from second to third base. The outfielders keep a wide distance between themselves. The relief pitchers are in a bullpen, often located behind the center field fence, over four hundred feet from the batter's box.

And the Pirates are truly adept at social distancing. They've been keeping themselves twenty or thirty games away from the first-place team for years!

The fans have been doing their part, too, especially by washing hands and wearing masks. If you're a Pirates fan, you've been washing your hands of your team's ninety-plus loss seasons now for some time. Every catcher wears a mask, but the Pirates' catcher and the masks worn by the fans might be worn over their collective noses to help prevent the stink from all those losing seasons as much as to protect against a virus.

No, this is nothing to joke about. Then again, at a time like this, what better tonic is there than a dash of humor?

Still, win or lose, I wanted to be at Opening Day again in 2020. My plans were curtailed, and even if the opener happens in, say, June, it won't be the same. All the tulips have sprung up by then. It sure would be nice to catch pennant fever this year rather than the fever of the coronavirus. But that doesn't sound too likely from what preseason prognosticators are projecting. They don't view the Pirates as "essential workers."

Oh well, maybe it's time the team goes into quarantine. You don't get much joy from a fist bump anyway. For this virus, let's all pray for a vaccine. For this baseball season, maybe it's time to pray for rain.

Take Me Out to the Ballgame . . . Someday!

The coronavirus pandemic has extinguished the lives of thousands in the United States and around the globe. Millions upon millions have been shoved into unemployment, many for the first time in their lives. We have all been shuttered at home for weeks that have turned into months.

As a society, we're trying to balance social distancing, mask-wearing, how often we should wash our hands, when can we go outside, when can we go to church again, how can we feed our families, when we can work again, when we can ramp up testing, and when will we have a vaccine. Not to mention when on earth can I get a haircut, although the entire pandemic experience is enough to make you pull your hair out.

But at least for me, and probably millions of others, there's a big void that continues to go unfilled. There is no baseball. How can this be? No baseball! When a virus like this strikes us down, have you noticed how much we start missing the little things? The things we have taken for granted for so long? This dawned on me the other day as I was taking my daily walk through my neighborhood as prescribed by my cardiologist. I am now two years removed from quadruple heart bypass surgery, and so I walk . . . every day. Now that I can't go anywhere because of the virus, the walks are no problem at all.

You see, it isn't a baseball game per se that I miss. It's everything surrounding it. The sights, sounds, and scents of baseball are ubiquitous by nature. I miss seeing grass so green in the outfield that it resembles St. Patrick's Day in Dublin. I miss the crack of the bat as it meets the ball, which then is lofted high toward the heavens against a bright blue sky. Heck, I even miss the organ rendition of that corny, worn-out song played by the Cavalry as they chased the American Indians.

I miss the scent of popcorn, grilled hot dogs, and sausage covered in stadium mustard. I miss the usher yelling out that he has cold beer . . . even if it will cost me twelve dollars. What I'd give to pay for a cold one right now! Any other season, any other time, I wouldn't be caught dead shelling out that much cash for a beer. Funny how our perspective can change, isn't it?

I miss watching people who are total strangers passing down someone's change for that twelve-dollar beer because the buyer gave the usher a ten and a five. I miss watching kids do silly dances to the Village People during the seventh inning stretch, fireworks going off when the home team clobbers a home run to dead center field, and a crowd of thirty-five thousand booing the umpire, unafraid of gathering in a large group.

I miss seeing a young father seated with his son at his first live baseball game, teaching him how to keep score. I miss people listening to their radios (or their phones nowadays) to hear the broadcast of the game they are watching in person. I miss baseball trivia questions on the scoreboard, reliving great moments on specific dates in a team's history, and the last two words of the national anthem: *"Play ball!"*

It's all gone now, and I wonder when a simpler time and simple pleasures will return. What's worse is that nobody, not even the esteemed Dr. Fauci, seems to know for sure.

And so, we wait. We wait like relief pitchers in a bullpen for that chance to take the field and wiggle our team out of an eighth-inning jam. Except there is no jam. Nobody is on base, and the bullpen is quiet, devoid of yet another sound, the one you can hear when a ninety-eight-mile-per-hour fastball explodes into a round, leather catcher's mitt.

None of these experiences will solve the coronavirus crisis. Certainly, none of them will bring back the lives our nation has lost. But it would provide us with some measure of joy and peace, a rekindling of all those wonderful moments we've overlooked and taken for granted.

"Take me out to the ballgame. Take me out to the crowd. Buy me some peanuts and crackerjacks. I don't care if I ever get back!" Before now, that was just a corny baseball song everyone knew

even if they didn't follow baseball. I didn't think I'd ever see the day when everyone would be singing it at the top of their lungs.

Tomorrow Isn't Promised

Just before Christmas 2019, I lost my nephew and good friend, Edward, to cancer. This wasn't supposed to happen. Not like this. And not this soon.

Edward was fifty-four years old, and I can remember the night my sister, Kathy, brought him into this world. That's what gets to me most. Even though I'm eleven years older and I'm still here, Ed is gone.

I know I'm not supposed to ask why. But I'm human, damn it, and it's only natural.

Ed and I did not have much in common. In fact, the more I think about it, we were as different as can be in many ways.

That's one thing I'll say for men. Unlike women, we can go months or even years without speaking, writing, texting, or communicating in any form, and nobody gets upset over it. No one asks, "Where the hell have you been?" If you go that long without contacting a woman, you'll likely get twenty questions or comments about how you are self-centered and that you don't care about her anymore. Not so with guys. We all have that "I'll catch ya later" attitude.

I could go months without seeing my nephew. Then, once I saw him again, I could remind him about the time we went to a Pittsburgh Pirates game at Three Rivers Stadium, and we'd both enjoy a boisterous laugh on cue. We got stuck in traffic (what else is new in downtown Pittsburgh?), and we didn't get to the parking lot until the top of the first inning. The Pirates were playing the Giants that day, and Jeffrey Leonard had already blasted a three-run home run before we even got to the gate. Heck, I barely had time to lock the doors. By the time we reached our seats, San Francisco was ahead 5–0 in the first inning.

I remember Ed asking me, "We came all this way for this?" I just shrugged. "Well, at least we can get something good to eat somewhere after the game," he added, trying to pry my mind away from the Pirates' huge deficit with eight painful innings still to play. It was early, but we both knew the Pirates were not coming back to win. Not the Pirates of the 1980s anyway. But there was always Primanti Brothers or Eat 'N Park, which had a good salad bar. At that time, we couldn't find either of those places in Ohio.

Ed and I went to Pirates games almost every year, and every year, they lost. I mean, the Pirates must have been 0–12 or something like that when we went to see them play. When we went to see them in the early '90s, they finally did field good teams, but they still lost. Every year! I was disgruntled on the way home every time. No amount of great food was going to alter my mood. The Pirates are my team, and the annual losing would wear on me.

Ed was even-keel. He would say, "Hey, it's a good time anyway, even if they don't win." He was right. At the time, I thought it was easy for him to say that. Ed liked the Oakland A's, so he just enjoyed whatever we did together. But he was right. He was tell-

Me with my nephew Ed (left) on my wedding day in May 1990.

ing me how much he enjoyed spending time with his only uncle, but because I was fixated on how the Pirates' starting pitching was a disaster, I missed the point.

At the time, we were both young, and we never thought about a day when we wouldn't be able to attend a ballgame together. Or recite the script of the first *Jaws* movie together. Or spend the holidays together. Or play ball in the yard together. We didn't think about mortality when Ed was nineteen and I was thirty. He was more like a younger brother to me than a nephew.

Ed passed away less than two weeks before Christmas, but I will always have those memories. The most important one is that he drove sixteen hours up from Florida with his two kids in the car to see me in the hospital the day before I was scheduled to have four-way heart bypass surgery in April 2018.

Less than two years later, I flew to Florida to see him in the hospital. But Ed was unconscious when I arrived. He never knew I was there at his side. But I knew. He always did and said the right thing to me every year when we went to a Pirates game and they lost again and again. Now it was my turn to do the right thing.

Sometimes in life, you don't ask what you should do. You just do it. Hug your kids. If you have a chance to make up for twenty years that you didn't speak to a family member, mend the fences while you can. Enjoy the ballgame, even if the home team is getting crushed, because a day will come when you will no longer have the games or those cherished moments.

Don't make the mistake of waiting until a loved one is lying in a hospital bed, unable to communicate. You don't know how many tomorrows you have. Besides, tomorrow isn't promised to anyone.

What? No Baseball?

When the calendar flips from February to March, life officially begins. January has only a New Year's Eve kiss at midnight (that is, if you have someone to kiss) and February has the Super Bowl (that is, if your team is playing in it) and Valentine's Day (that is, if you have the aforementioned someone to kiss). But both months offer little else, save for icy road travel and snow piled so high you can't get out of your garage.

This brings us back to March. In March, we rise from our winter doldrums. Daylight savings kicks in, and the days get longer. In some years, Easter comes in March, and even if it doesn't, the anticipation of Easter is now close at hand. You start seeing the sun again, which has not been visible since October 20.

People start buying lawn equipment. Buds that will blossom into red tulips by June are no longer a rumor. Travelers embark for Florida, where March there feels like June or July here. The white sandy beaches, palm trees swirling in the warm winds, unrelenting waves off the Gulf, and sunsets that embrace the horizon as far as your eye can see make for lasting images on your iPhone that you could have sold as postcards at the drugstore in 1982.

Yet, something is missing. What could it be? It's always been here before. There's a baseball diamond as pure as the one Kevin Costner built in *Field of Dreams*. But now, we may have to wait until "Shoeless" Joe Jackson and his friends come charging out of a cornfield, or in Florida's case, maybe an orange grove.

That might be more of a possibility than waiting on today's Major League baseball players to occupy their positions on a pristine diamond. Baseball's owners and players are bogged down in a stalemate, and the players have been locked out. Each day that passes means more games are canceled. I don't know all the issues, and I don't care to know them. What I do know is that I'm going to Florida in March, the month when life begins anew, and there may not be baseball.

Of course, most reasonably adjusted and sound of mind individuals would say, "So what?" These people have vacationed in Florida for years, and the beach, sun, sand, shrimp, and parasailing were more than enough to attract them to head south. And for some, after experiencing all of those refreshing human delights, maybe they took in a baseball exhibition game in Bradenton, Sarasota, Clearwater, or Fort Myers . . . maybe. But that was not the reason they went there. They already got what they wanted.

Then there are people like me. Initially, I went down for baseball first and foremost, but later I discovered the beach, the sun, the sand, and the shrimp. I like all those things too, mind you. I relish the Shark on the Barbie served at Sharky's Seagrill on Gulf Drive, Bradenton Beach. Or the grouper served up at The Beachhouse, just a mile or so up the road. What's not to like?

But to say I go to Florida for all those experiences would be inaccurate. To me, there just needs to be baseball. It's like eating the food at a wedding reception, but you skipped the ceremony. Or you had your steak and baked potato but didn't stick around to hear the guest speaker talk about social security and saving for your retirement.

For me, baseball is the centerpiece of these trips, and if that's taken away, I'm scrambling to find something else to fill the void. As luck would have it, I may have found it for this year's excursion. Richard Marx, who had a string of Top 40 hits in the 1980s, will be performing while I'm in the area. Listening to his gifted voice belt out "Endless Summer Nights" will have to suffice because I may not have another available entertainment option. I'm looking forward to his performance, but without baseball this spring and maybe even this summer, there will indeed be "Endless Summer Nights."

This is a painful possibility, one that I do not wish on even my staunchest adversaries. If you don't suffer this affliction, you are luckier and smarter than me. You have successfully avoided pain that you didn't cause. But you have also missed out on a lot that would take me close to a lifetime to explain, like how Pirates lefthander Harvey Haddix lost a perfect game after pitching twelve immaculate innings one night in Milwaukee on May 26, 1959. But hey, there will still be the Gulf winds in your face, a tube of unused sun lotion, and a slice of Florida's famous key lime pie awaiting you.

Still, you won't hear the crack of the bat or a white sphere elevated against a bright blue sky. And while it's true that we don't miss what we've never experienced, for those of us who have, it remains a crying shame.

Sharky's Seagrill is a must visit every time I'm in town.

A Kid at Sixty-Five

Baseball is often described as a generational sport. Fathers pass the game down to their sons and daughters, who can one day do the same for their kids. However, sometimes you can find yourself passing a baseball experience along to someone younger . . . just not young enough to be your son.

I found myself in that situation on a hot summer Saturday afternoon in July. I drove two of my close pals to PNC Park in Pittsburgh for a game between the Pirates and Milwaukee Brewers. Both friends are named Dave—sixty-year-old Dave S. and sixty-five-year-old Dave W.

Dave S. and I have been venturing to see a game in Pittsburgh for several years now. But for Dave W., this was a brand-new baseball experience. You see, while Dave W. had seen many ballgames in Cleveland, never once had he ever seen a Pirates game in person. I've introduced many to that "first-time" experience of Pirates baseball, and Dave W. has become the latest person who can now officially cross that off his bucket list.

I saw my first Pirates game when I was fifteen. Dave W. saw his first at age sixty-five. When you go to a ball game with friends and the home team wins, as they did on this afternoon with a 7–4 Pirates victory, it makes you feel like a youngster again. For a few hours, I could watch a sixty-five-year-old man who is nearing retirement, a man who still carries parental responsibilities at this stage of his life, sit back and seem as though his worries and concerns were a galaxy away.

That's the sense a ballgame can give you. It doesn't matter what ballpark you go to. It doesn't matter who your favorite team is or if you even have a favorite. What matters is who you are with to experience it. I, of course, enjoyed the day, too. But I've seen the Pirates play hundreds of games by now, so I was far more interested in what Dave W. thought. How did he like it? What impressed him most?

Turns out, it was no surprise. Many first-timers say they mostly like the view of the Pittsburgh skyline from their PNC Park seat. That was Dave W.'s first reaction, too, although that observation seems somewhat perplexing. Remember, Dave W. is a staunch Cleveland fan of both the Guardians and the Browns, so for him to say he liked even a cobblestone on Stanwix Street would be a noteworthy comment. I don't think either of my friends named Dave knew many of the Pirates batters who came to the plate on this day. This is a very young Pittsburgh team, and even I have to make sure I spell their names correctly in my scorebook. Yes, I still keep score, a lost art among fans today.

Michael Chavis and rookie sensation Oneil Cruz belted home runs on this day. By the seventh inning of a game that started at 4:05 p.m., both Daves were secretly wondering where we were going to have dinner! (Okay, I admit I thought that myself, even if I was the only one dressed in Pirates gear.)

Pirates attire is so foreign to Dave W. that he had to scrounge up a yellow T-shirt to wear to the game. Cleveland fans wearing black and yellow is like asking Lady Gaga to dress in a nun's habit!

Who cares if we didn't get back home to Ohio until after eleven? We are all in our sixties, and nobody has a curfew anymore. Both Daves are married guys, so if anyone would have a curfew, it would be them, not me. Being single, I won't get a text on the turnpike that says, "Hey honey . . . you okay? What time will you be home, sweetie?"

That's okay. On a day like this one, all of us were kids again . . . even for just a few hours.

On the Clemente bridge with my friend Dave Waseity (right), July 2022. It was Dave's first Pirates' baseball game!

Baseball, Marriage, and Family

When Bill Mazeroski hit a ninth-inning home run in Game Seven of the 1960 World Series, a lot more happened than just the Pirates beating the Yankees to win baseball's top prize. Most of us saw Mazeroski hit a high fastball over the left field wall off New York's Ralph Terry at Forbes Field that autumn day of October 13.

Irene Abel saw a lot more. A Pittsburgh resident, Irene, or 'Rene as she is called, was working downtown when "Maz" connected for his historic blast. She had attended Game Two of the Series that year, a 16–3 blowout victory for the Bronx Bombers. "I didn't get a ticket for the seventh game," she recalls. "It was only about five dollars, but most of us didn't think the World Series would go that far." Indeed, the Yankees were a prohibitive favorite to win the Fall Classic in either four, five, or at most, six games.

But it went the full seven games, and when Mazeroski homered at 3:36 that afternoon, Irene Abel's life would change forever. "I was working as a key punch operator, and when the Pirates won, everyone stopped working. They threw their computer tapes and papers out the window. They closed the office and walked out."

Irene, now eighty-five, said she phoned a couple of her girlfriends and asked them to round up some guys they knew to go out and celebrate. Pittsburgh was awash in papers, confetti and streamers everywhere in the downtown streets. "There were people sitting on the tops of cars riding around. There were parties and celebrations going on everywhere," Irene recalled. "You couldn't drive through town. There was so much paper in the streets."

Her girlfriends did contact some guys, and their plan was to pick up the three girls.

One of them was Enos Abel, who drove a red and white 1955 Chevrolet. That was when Irene met Enos. "We ended up at the Cork & Bottle restaurant. He called me three days later, and we went out on a date. We got engaged exactly one year later, on October 13, 1961. We were married for fifty-seven years."

Each year on October 13, a crowd gathers at "The Wall" in Oakland, a suburban neighborhood near the University of Pittsburgh, the site where Forbes Field once stood before it was leveled in 1972. The group relives Game Seven on that day each year, listening to the entire broadcast as it was delivered on the radio in 1960. A collection of enthusiasts called the Game Seven Gang has been responsible for making the commemoration possible each year since 1992. And each year, Irene Abel attends. While in a wheelchair, she receives assistance from her daughter, Lynne Abel VandenBosche, age fifty-four. Enos attended each year as well until he passed away in 2014.

Lynne stepped back for a second, just before the start of the broadcast of Game Seven. "You know," she said, "if Mazeroski wouldn't have hit the home run to win the World Series, I'd have never been born!"

Here's the moral of the story: the next time somebody says baseball is boring and that all you're doing is watching one guy throw a ball and another guy standing there trying to hit it with a stick in his hand, remind them there's a lot more going on than meets the eye. Courtship, marriage, and family might come to be due to a baseball game.

That day, Mazeroski didn't strike out. Neither did Irene Abel, who would meet the love of her life.

Thanks, Dad!

There are many times when I think about my father, but especially each year on Father's Day. I have many memories of him that had nothing to do with baseball, but what I realized years after he passed is that the baseball memories I do have with him exist because of his unselfishness, his willingness to take notice of what interested me, and what stirred my passions, not his own.

Three clear occurrences stand out regarding baseball with Dad. The first was when he would buy my sister Chris and me a box of baseball cards and bring them home on a Friday afternoon after working over eight hours at a factory job. Wow! That's generous, right?

Ah, but here's the catch: we didn't get the whole box of cards at once. Instead, we'd get one pack a week, with only five cards in a pack.

Furthermore, we'd only get those five if, and I mean IF, we were on good behavior at home with Mom. If not, we were stuck looking at the same five guys for another week. And we must have gotten a Harvey Haddix baseball card thirty-five times!

So why couldn't we just have reached up on top of the refrigerator to grab a handful of packs, you ask? Well, for one thing, when you're five years old, you can't reach that high. My sister was older and taller and could have fetched a step stool, but it wasn't a risk worth taking. If your mom was like our mom, she had 20/20 telescopic vision, along with binoculars that grew from her ears. There would be no getting past her.

Eventually, we got to open all the baseball cards in the box, but more importantly, we learned the value of patience. Nothing you desire should ever come without effort, without some sacrifice.

Our summer vacation as children also came with an annual drive to Cleveland to see the Indians play. My first major league game came in 1958 when I saw the legendary Jimmy Piersall literally sit down in center field in a game against the Baltimore Orioles. If Piersall wasn't getting any fly balls in his direction and the batter continued to foul off pitches, he simply took it upon himself to plop down on the blades of grass in Cleveland Stadium.

Then there was the time Dad bought me a "pitch back" for my birthday one year. This was a squared device with a mesh net across it. It would retrieve the ball back to you once you threw it into the net. That helped me learn which way to turn my glove to accept throws. It came in handy as I prepared to play second base in Little League that year.

You see, Dad never knew every player on every team. He never collected baseball cards. He couldn't have told you who won the World Series ten years ago or who won the Cy Young Award last season. He didn't know the players on my favorite team, the Pirates. His team was the Indians, and while he wrote beautiful poetry, as far as I know, he never wrote a word about baseball.

What he did, however, was far more important. He knew that baseball and sports in general were important to his kids, and he made sure he supported our interests as we were growing up.

You know that quote, "Anybody can be a father, but it takes someone special to be a Dad"? Boy, that sure applied to him. Learning which way to turn your glove is something essential that we all need to learn in life. You realize it suddenly one day when you look up and see what's coming toward you.

Shaking hands with my dad. What I'd give to do that just one more time!

This Old House

The inevitable finally happened. My sisters—and to a lesser extent, myself—faced what we knew someday would come to pass. We were moving from our two-story family home as my sisters looked to downsize into a smaller house more suitable to their current household needs.

Built in 1928, this was our parents' home. However, they have passed on, and the three of us were now faced with this difficult, yet understandable and inevitable decision. We moved into This Old House when I was just six months old in 1955, and now it was time to leave.

Most of my assistance in the move involved taking old clothes, household items, and old records to various venues that would accept them. Taking out old albums and 45 records of Gordon Lightfoot, The Moody Blues, and even ones I never listened to, like Sergio Franchi, Johnny Mathis, or Bobby Goldsboro, was hard enough, as it represented another severed branch from my youth.

What was even harder to handle was all the intangibles. All the Pirates games I listened to on Mom's Magnavox in the kitchen and on the front, side, and back porches—not to mention the garage, the living room near her Victorian chairs, and the basement. I can still vividly recall hearing Willie Stargell's home run on the back patio as Dad grilled hot dogs and hamburgers on Memorial Day, 1971. The Pirates ripped the Cubs that day, 10–0 at Three Rivers Stadium.

Every person has their own memories. I have mine. My memories can't be anyone else's, and they can never be taken away. Baseball makes a much greater impression on you during your adolescence. Not only do I remember Stargell's home run that day, but I remember where on the patio I was standing when he hit it. I also recall Bob Prince describing it on KDKA. "And there's a ball hit very deep to right center field . . . You can spread some 'Chicken on the Hill' with Will!" In those days, Stargell operated a chicken house in Pittsburgh's Hill District. Every time he hit a home run, whoever was in the restaurant at that time received a free bucket of chicken.

Even if the Pirates of the future hit a big home run on a holiday, it will not have the same imprint on me now that I live in a two-bedroom apartment, or in the new ranch home my sisters moved to. Sure, it might make a big impression on someone else. But for me, it just won't leave the same lasting memory as the one Stargell belted on May 30, 1971.

This Old House of ours sure has many, many memories. If only it could speak, what a story it would tell. All the priests my mother served spaghetti and meatballs to, the tax and insurance papers we all poured over at the kitchen table, all the girlfriends I brought home for my parents to meet, the band I sang in during high school when we performed on the driveway for friends and family on my sixteenth birthday, how I used to pretend the ivy on our brick walls was easily the equal of Chicago's Wrigley Field, mowing the lawn, front and back while my Dad trimmed the hedges, the lessons he gave me in the garage on where the gas and oil went in the lawnmower and how to start it up. Or, the lasting image of my grandfather walking down the driveway with the assistance of a cane.

You can't make up these memories. You can't replace them. And yet, nobody can ever take them away.

My grandfather, Giacomo DiCola, takes a stroll down the drive of This Old House.

Acknowledgments

I thank the following influential people in my life for making this book possible:

Thank you, Mom and Dad, for the way you raised me and the lessons you taught. Thank you, Dad, for teaching me the value of the written word. Thank you, Mom, for your Magnavox radio, the title of this book, and teaching me how to engage the public.

Thank you to my sisters, Chris and Kathy—Chris for finding that Robin Roberts baseball card on the school bus and countless hours playing catch in the yard, and Kathy for giving me tips on how to catch the girl I had my eye on.

Thank you to my nephew Edward and all those trips we made together to Three Rivers Stadium and PNC Park.

Thank you, Charlie Bowersox, for being our family life insurance agent and calling out to me one summer day in 1976: "Hey, you want to write something for me?" Hence, my sports writing career was officially launched.

Thank you to Kori Frazier Morgan for

"cleaning up my act!" A lot of time and attention to detail goes into a project such as this. Thank you, Kori!

Thank you to Ryan Humbert for creating this book's amazing cover, as well as Charlie Edmisten for taking photographs of my prized baseball possessions.

Thanks also to Mr. Paul Clapper, past editor of The Herald newspaper in Louisville, Ohio. Mr. Clapper once told me, "You get me your sports story by the deadline each week, and I'll run it." That was over forty years ago!

Lastly, thank you, Kora Sadler, founder of the Akron, Ohio Writers Group, for always believing in me and that this book would one day become a reality, even when I had serious doubts I could do it.

About the Author

A baseball enthusiast all his life, Ben DiCola has the programs, scorecards, ticket stubs, photos, and thousands of baseball cards to prove it. He saw his first baseball game at age four in Cleveland Stadium, but it's his memories and fascination with Forbes Field in Pittsburgh that have stood the test of time for over sixty years.

Ben has also spent over forty years as a sportswriter/photographer in his hometown of Canton, Ohio covering high school football, basketball, baseball, volleyball, and track for various schools and newspapers including the *Massillon Independent, Louisville Herald, North Canton Sun Journal,* and *Alliance Review* and has had business articles published by the *Akron Beacon Journal*. He has also written sports and human interest stories for *Akron Life* and the former *Stark Magazine.*

Outside of the print medium, Ben has been on the radio airwaves, broadcasting both news and sports on WNYN Canton, WSLR Akron, and WHBC Canton. This is Ben's maiden book, where he brings together his family life and those closest to him with his favorite sport growing up. He hopes you will enjoy it, and if a tear comes to your eye while reading one page, maybe it will be replaced by a chuckle on the next.